STAGE DESIGN

D1245288

STAGE

DESIGN

HOWARD BAY

DRAMA BOOK SPECIALISTS / PUBLISHERS

Library of Congress Cataloging in Publication Data

Bay, Howard.
   Stage design.

    1. Theaters—Stage-setting and scenery.
2. Moving-pictures—Setting and scenery. 3. Television
—Stage-setting and scenery. I. Title.
PN2091.S8B325   791   73-15948
ISBN 0-910482-46-2

Printed in U.S.A. by
NOBLE OFFSET PRINTERS, INC.
New York, N.Y. 10003

DEDICATED TO:

Bobby Clark, Bert Lahr, Joe Frisco, Bozo Snyder, Jerzy Grotowski, Bea Lillie, Ethel Merman, J. J. Grandville, Gustave Dore, Max Ernst, Saul Steinberg, Inigo Jones, Robert Edmond Jones, Albert Johnson, The Scenic Artists of America, Rodgers & Hart, Cole Porter, Frank Loesser, George Abbott, Lillian Hellman, Strindberg, George Jean Nathan, Hallie Flanaghan, Helen Tamiris, Herman Shumlin, Albert Marre, Lem Ward, Kaufman & Hart, Michael Todd, Ellen Stewart, Kermit Bloomgarden, Frederick Law Olmsted, John Paxton, A. J. Davis, Mary Martin, Mu Chí, N. C. Wyeth, Torelli, H. Bosch, H. Pinter, Hassard Short, Vincent Sardi Senior, Billie Holiday, Thomas Edison, Atget, Gaudi, and with a special dedication to Ruth Bay.

CONTENTS

STAGE DESIGN

I.
The Theatrical Climate & Dramatic Design

Once upon a time our most eminent American scenic designer composed an epistle to the Young Stage Designer beseeching him to take off on flights of Imagination, on Wings of Song, and not to fall prey to the siren call of the Ribboned Jezebels of the marketplace. I really don't think that is our problem right now. Finding the residue of the theatrical marketplace is a bit tricky, coming across a young hopeful from River City with portfolio attached, "Gee, Mr. Merrick, if I could only get a shot at that Champion musical," you must stay up for the Late, Late Show. In the words of Nunnally Johnson to his son preparing for the Broadway-Hollywood circuit, "Scott, I am afraid you are frantically trying to get a last-minute reservation on the Titanic." Today we are exposed to a flood of cliches that smother discussion of our sad theatre. The embryo designer has a trying time sorting out his or her thoughts and making a stab at charting a life work. The bromides are ground out in equal quantities by the senior citizens with their In-My-Day-Plays-Were-Plays and the avant-garde promoters with their On-To-The-Nonliterary-Unstructured-Tomorrow. From Scenery-Never-Sold-Any-Tickets to Abbie Hoffman-Is-Theatre-Now, a body doesn't know which way to turn. For instance, everybody says that People In The Theatre Are Dedicated. I suppose that is as true as any fat pronouncement, but I am going to be surly and ask: To What Are We Dedicated? Take your time;

don't answer Dedicated To The Theatre or we won't get anywhere. That could range from supporting Neil Simon in the style to which he has become accustomed to filling out the dog days with yet another revival of *The Fantasticks*. Or erecting a funny building with half timbering pasted on it in Stratford, Connecticut, and dressing Shakespeare in Carnaby Street. And Self-Expression is definitely off target because that can interest only one person and immediate family. Dedication connotes something beyond procuring groceries for oneself and Loved Ones. And Preserving the Classics, Bringing Real Art To The People, is back with Baskets For The Poor at Yuletide. Dedication has something to do with Goals—heading in a particular direction that is deemed important. The American Theatre is fresh out of Goals; the flicker of hope is that we are beginning to notice it.

We are inundated by cultural press releases dressing up the paltry hits; the loyal opposition critics of the weeklies spin elite fantasies about Third Theatre, relevant revivals and other tasteful bagatelles. Daylight never enters the salon; it does remind me to renew my subscription to *Hound and Horn*. Even more pixilated is the fearless verbiage of the Paradise Now Crowd: you too can achieve instant freedom; shed your garments and join hands; no messy, irritating craft or social problems. Call your local group leader now. We must chop through the glut of balmy words that derail the apprentice designer from concentrating on rationally ordering his talent and knowledge. The designer in the process of taking shape faces a more bewildering prospect than other students of the drama, because the available texts are woefully dated on two counts: (1) They accept *a priori* the philosophy of pictorial embellishments of the fading traditional stage. (2) They are further removed from life by being put together by out-of-touch academicians—even if they throw in shots of real Broadway shows and the insides of real scenic studios. The recipes for making ordinary scenery catalogued in Burris-Meyer and Cole's *Scenery for the Theatre* (Little Brown) and Parker and Smith's *Scene Design and Stage Lighting* (Holt, Rinehart and Winston) service the designer-technicians marooned far from knowledgeable mechanics and regular shops. Then there are the untidy masses of arts and crafts that the stage designer must grapple with, and since the very premises of aesthetics are up for grabs, the confusion is almost beyond repair. Is the dragged-out apprenticeship in the backstage disciplines still a necessary trip if those disciplines were made to service a passing epoch in theatre history? Is science, with its slides and films and electronic know-how, automatically a dazzling assist? Do street theatre, guerrilla theatre and that looming Third World theatre really require the helping hand of your friendly half-inch-scale water-colorist? Or that utterly boorish query: Is the theatre sinking to a high-toned training camp for the giants of the entertainment industry? Oh yes, and with the economy going to pot, we all know what is jettisoned first, don't we? Has anyone heard if they have turned off the phone down there at the American National Theatre and Academy?

The next question on the agenda: Is There a Crying Need for Kindergarten Chats from one of the Elder Practitioners of Scenic Art? We have hinted that the quaint How-To-Build-a-Flat cookbooks reflect little awareness of modern work habits either on the drawing board, in the shops or backstage. With straight faces they proceed to illustrate Alfred Jarry's quip delivered in 1896: "There are two kinds of decor, interiors and exteriors." The rhapsodic tone poems for the Theatre Unbound that are still on the library shelves are of little guidance. And the Do-It-Yourself kit of slides, strobe and spray cans for disposable events is amateur night at the student union. Scanty illumination is furnished by the marginal references to scenery in the manifestoes of the New Theatre.

What compels me to write is pure, wide-eyed faith in the talent and promise of the next generation of scenic artists, because by and large they are a thinking lot. The presumptive corollary is that I can help pack them off on the right path—if we can just find the compass. This new batch of design-technical students is not panting to conquer the Great White Way (though like Mount Everest, It Is There); they aren't that keen about the prospect of bondage to the resident companies that are hanging on by their dentures; and they feel a bit beyond the medieval scholars still holding the bastions of higher learning. They do desire to be members of vital theatre collectives, combines that rassle with live dramatic stuff. The catch is that unlike actors and directors and playwrights, who walk around with their built-in crafts, designers are impotent without monies for physical production. The bouncing drama groups are short on cash and with backward theorizing construct elaborate rationales for foregoing visual dressing. This too shall pass as the healthier outfits grow up and reach for audiences beyond the camp-followers.

Actors are the primary element, the given quantity, but designers are the craftsmen embedded in the workings of stage creation. It must mean something that the three signpost books on the large periods of modern American theatre were written by designers. The thesis presented here is that these periods are washed up, but the refurbished and retooled designer will furnish the spine of stagecraft, the continuity of theatre styles. We must codify the living tradition to arm tomorrow's designers. The need is not fulfilled by the quantitative piling up of technical wizardry, and certainly not by laying end to end the fascinating anecdotes from My Life in the Theatre. Nor will a sumptuous picture book of prime examples of stage embellishments throughout the world suffice. The secret has leaked out—the theatre is in transition, to put it mildly. The news that the Renaissance is dead has reached Shubert Alley and its passing has triggered unsettling implications for the Drama As We Know It. To make matters worse, that hopeful cultural appendage, the Regional Repertory Company, isn't in too good shape since the first bloom of Civic Pride and Foundation Support faded away. Our Classic Inheritance has lost its charm; Grace and Beauty are remainder items. The well-made play is filed under "Revivals, Summer Stock." The onward and upward march of the Drama toward the Wagnerian ideal of the perfect blending of the Arts in an indivisible, unfocalized emotional orgy doesn't seem worthwhile any more. Only a few seasons back there was talk about the Human Condition, and the words Archetype and Myth were bandied about as if there were some large constants in behaviour operating unchanged since the primeval ooze days. As I say, this was a few seasons ago. It hasn't been very helpful to chase the birth of theatre back to primitive rituals as we are not equipped with strong beliefs in anything right now, and ritual demands monolithic beliefs from the populace. Beyond the obvious signs of upheaval, such as the waning of playwrights as unlicensed psychiatrists and the shrivelling of all the petty little tragedies and little comedies, the entire underpinnings have slithered out from under dramaturgy—just can't cope with a blandly insane world. Let us not make the terrible mistake that stories about human beings are going out of style. What has happened is that large genres have passed on—not only the Tennis Anyone? but the low-calorie Freud, the costume pageants with Important Personages as Ordinary Folks Like You and Me, the plastic sit-coms, the tender young hero against the crass world, etc. Focus has shifted to new people-problems, but dramatists have not invented forms to freeze the disaster bulletins. Architecture will rescue the theatre. That's it! Erase that gold frame, that baroque symbol of dead royalty, and unleash the actor. Well anyway . . . we encourage playwrights if we interest some foundation . . . . Playwrights, ach—who needs them? The band of improvising souls who will set up shop on any street corner, in the subways, and throw in a late show in the church basement . . . . No, actors are hung up on self-conscious, moldy, artificial training—it's all Too Structured. Happenings passed through with fanfare; something sublime will spontaneously come to pass if only attuned, Beautiful People can blend in an Event—if the stars are right . . . .

All very refreshing, quantities of garbage have been carted away. But there is a large hole for all the brave whistling in the dark. Forgetting the Self-Fulfillment Groupies—which is easy to do—what positive, concrete theatrical forms are likely to fill the vacuum? Because even a lowly manual on scenery must be geared to what will be pertinent a few years hence. Physical production, the visual arm of theatre, is all unstuck too. The new landscape in art, the new media and the new playwriting demand attention as we plunge into the practical business of design. Otherwise we would find that we had outlined the manifold uses of the stone ax in the era of the computer. Only one thought which I will repeat ad nauseam: The student designer-technician must acquire academic drawing skill and imbibe all the mechanical knowledge the modern shops and craftsmen have to offer. It is wise to learn to handle the best available tools because the precise form of the coming theatre is mighty hazy. Not so many years ago I was saddened by a journey through America's art schools and college art departments. Abstract expressionists were being turned out by the gross, and it didn't take any awesome prophesy on my part to foretell the demise of abstract expressionism. If all those out-of-date young painters had been taught grubby drawing, they could have shifted gears and meshed in with the next fashion in paintbrush wielding. The moral is that theatre never has been nor ever will be limited to one style but is as varied as life itself (a tasteful motto to hang over your drawing board).

It would be nice to uplift this rambling preface with a clarion call for beauty and truth, but I fear there is no great call for beauty at the moment, and truth has changed hands so often lately that she may as well shack up with last year's recording star—what with residuals and all. Glamor isn't a drug on the market, it just isn't around. Here we go with another scintillating Noel Coward revival while a couple of evergreens in northwestern Montana haven't felt the smog yet. *Crazy* used to be a moderately handy word, but it shouldn't be put in every sentence, should it? Dear Young Designer: I know you are going to persist in this weird undertaking. But along with all the useful information about hardware and resistance dimmers that you are going to sop up in the following pages, as a favor, please notice what is going on with the Private People (that, naturally, is how we refer to everyone outside the amusement industry). You may find you won't be so flabbergasted by the sudden somersaults of the Entertainment World—if you will excuse the expression.

As my colleagues in academe would say, stylistically the writing leaves something to be desired. It is just that I have never been able to overcome a childhood of George Ade's *Fables in Slang* and the King James version of the Good Book, formative years at Sardi's bar, and to top that off, a prolonged dose of Mike Todd. I do think I have shown commendable restraint by skipping juicy tales of theatre folk. If I have interlarded discussions of nuts and bolts with some disrespectful jabs at shoddy practices in the centers of commerce, it is for Your Own Good. Students who have been out in the battlefield for a while complain that no one in school covered unions and unscrupulous producers. You will note the brusque treatment meted out to imagination and creativity and other lofty subjects—a deliberate snub calculated to offset the customary self-indulgent, highly tinted presentation of theatre-making. Creativity will blossom against all odds; inspirational words laid end to end will not hasten its growth. I have chosen to pound away at the neglected prerequisites for a functioning designer: seeing the physical world fresh and clear; using the total brain to concretize a production concept; drawing and drawing and drawing in a literal, unfashionable fashion; tracking down all materials and processes than can help the drama. So there is little talk of imagination and creativity; they don't come about by talk anyway. First one should learn to draw and know which is stage right.

But there is a Larger Design, as the preacher used to say. The Arts breeze along in a cocoon of their own devising. There is chatter about Relevance, but it is solved by hiring one or two from the vocal minorities or dispatching a spiffy mobile theatre with nursery level Commedia dell'Arte to the Under-Privileged. Public Relations is so anesthetizing that no one is disturbed that one of The Art Critics prattles away on a retainer from the C.I.A. or asks just why did Radical Theatre X drag down a comfy foundation grant. The theatre is not as bluntly manipulated by the Taste Makers as Some Arts We Know but it is as separated from the American population as the Pentagon. The theatre's isolation from the world out there may not be noticed by the young designer until late in the day, and I shall explain why. There is no record of the creation of an instant designer; the breeding of designers is a dragged-out process marked by an obsessive concentration on Technique, because the end product is an amalgam of countless specialized skills. The designer fabricates the concrete world wherein the actors live out their fictional lives. The range of history and geography ordered by the dramatist demands an eclectic, multifaceted artist-craftsman. The designer's cranium is the busy intersection between Showbiz and the Finer Arts—stuffed with the debris of Man's building and crafts from the Dawn of History. The designer is the short-order chef who lifts the artifacts germane to a single theatre piece—the scraps of dead architecture, workaday accessories, technical contrivances and artificial lights—and welds them into an organic whole illuminating the drama, all within the budget and on schedule.

The Real Snapper is that this exhaustive apprenticeship is an amalgam of data and attitudes peculiar to a theatre that may well fade into the Scrapbook of History by the time the young hopeful graduates and composes his first résumé for prospective employers. The slick, uncritical pictorialism—the ocular Muzak—that has cluttered up the stages of the Western World for these many seasons may not be in demand—the designer may find himself the plaintive soulmate of the anvil salesman in The Music Man. No need to labor the point, Broadway has lost the Mecca franchise. So the question is how we gird our loins and battle the Great Unknown. It calls for a two-pronged attack. The potential designer must bestir himself, crawl out of the pages of Variety (and The Drama Review for that matter, and Sight and Sound, now that you mention it) and keep up with the goings on out there where people get up in the morning and go to work—things like that. The Hardhats on the Rampage was the best invention since the Bloody Mary for waking up the dreamers. One must finally grasp the thought that the theatre a decade hence will be forced to reach out and bring joy and excitement to an awful lot of people who don't read John Simon and don't care whether Lope de Vega is ensconced in Gotham playhouses. The chilling fact is that the choice will not be between Cactus Flower and a posh revival but whether any dramatic effort can be constructed that interests many hitherto indifferent voters. The most idiotic stance is that audiences *should* patronize our elevated works of art. So the coming designer would be advised to have his antennae out for the whole raucous panorama of popculture—and don't dissipate a month's allowance on that lovely Beaton drawing.

Now for the other Wing of the offensive, a responsibility that falls on this little brochure. On the negative side I have skipped lengthy theorizing on bygone "isms" in scenic design because at this juncture they tend to melt together. One-time fierce opponents begin to appear rather chummy as the naturalism versus symbolism furor slides back into perspective; they were surface variations of the very same philosophical stand. Half the struggle is giving the proper weight to information that has a fighting chance of being usable after the design student is sprung out of the classroom, and ruthlessly squashing the temptation to include attractive but dying stuff. Words have lost their age-old meanings, and since words have always been painfully inadequate in dealing with fugitive scenic art, I have crammed in a multitude of pictures.

Woven throughout the details hopefully tailored for tomorrow's needs are Inspiring Wall Mottoes for the Young Designer. Choice samples: (1) Design is not an adornment; it is the visual progression of a dramatic event. (2) Style is concept; not a peculiar way of drawing. (3) Technique is neutral. All techniques are of equal value. Pipe scaffolding plus beat-up styrofoam is not automatically superior to painted canvas; an antimacassar may be more appropriate than shiny mylar. (4) Technique must become second nature—the Zen archery bit. (5) The only security blanket for the jittery theatrical weather is a philosophy pieced together outside the stage door—philosophy is not handled by the William Morris Agency. (6) Designers are more apt to find inspiration in a horrendous Supermarket than in a smoothie Madison Avenue gallery.

The crusading tomes that flowered in the '20s are still with us through recent reprints, and your young minds can now be warped and twisted as ours were with naturalism, illusionism, expressionism, neo-realism, selective realism, constructivism, etc., etc. Then the published efforts thinned out to three widely spaced books by American designers: Robert Edmond Jones's evangelical essay, *The Dramatic Imagination;* Lee Simonson's cold shower for the soaring words, *The Stage Is Set,* a polemic for the designer as humble craftsman in the service of the Great Playwright To Come, was superseded by Mordecai Gorelik's *New Theatres for Old.* Max rather lugubriously nailed down the historical roots of scenic design and introduced Brecht to the States. It is a book that was years ahead of its time.

That was in 1940 and here we are in the 1970s. The embryo designer bombarded by the screaming media is reduced to a shivering, lonely body with no shared credo for warmth and sustenance. Not a unique predicament in this Year of Grace, but it is extra-rough in the dramatic design line because of the glut of arts and crafts and technical impedimenta involved.

This project is an uneasy mixture in a fundamental sense. There are two devils to vanquish. One is the frenetic piling up of time-honored backstage trivia that are never examined before use. The other is the pall of hazy, inspirational writing on the art of scenic design that takes years to clear out of the brain. We must oscillate between striving for the big perspective on practical training, while hammering out a logical theoretical approach to our lunatic craft. This schizoid format is an honest blend of my own professional and teaching lives.

On one hand, we must delineate the timeworn process of the designer creating and following through his creations, and accompanying this we are honor-bound to carry news of current equipment. I have skipped the schoolbook words and pictures describing just how to make each and every piece of conventional scenery because even the most explicit and detailed instructions fall short. No scenic element is an exact duplicate of some classic prototype. No student has learned how to turn out the fixin's for a show without the personal guidance of an expert stage mechanic. Such a categorical statement derives from a close acquaintance with the M.F.A. audition portfolios of the products of American university drama departments. The Substantive Issue to which we shall address ourselves in these pages (as we phrase it within the Halls of Ivy) is the indoctrination of a professional approach to the total field of theatrical design. Our perusal of technical matter is aimed at building the *designer's* overall grasp of the execution of his creations—nothing else. Beyond the stockpiling of work patterns pertinent to Broadway and its cut-rate copies is our mission to break out of this tabulation of the status quo and prepare our charges for a world in flux. It may get a bit hairy and the synthesis may come to pass long after closing this volume and after hassling the real theatre for a spell.

I shall close on a flashback to World War II when I seem to have furnished the dressing for all the bloated musicals with "Girls" in the titles. Many of these gems were underwritten with the gains from illicit operations. Brigands disguised as managers latched onto the freewheeling spenders and aided and abetted spectacle that was junked prior to opening. Of course, kickbacks were never unscrambled by attorney generals short on publicity. The borderline was always fuzzy between the deceptively simple story line of the decent musical and the inane tale meandering through a dizzy song-and-dance confection. The crummy entrepreneurs strung together idiot Production Numbers, variations on Miss Natural Resources in another Exotic Locale. That was the heyday of the fake romantic ruins; the Bibienas ending up as some doughy cupids and a busted column. While the junior gangsters were cavorting with the dames of the chorus, the perspiring designers were striving to give the stage a neat, crisp look to offset the soiled jokes—creating, as it were, the Total Environment for the Rhinestone Navel. The most palatable of this ga-ga pastry was the handiwork of the Last of the Red-Hot Showmen, those neo-Barnums, Billy Rose and Mike Todd. Those exuberant pirates operated on the Hegelian theory that quantity is transformed into quality. Rose was impressed with culture, which occasionally got him into trouble, but not Todd, who kept his eye on the Big Entertainment Values. He gave them Meat and Potato Shows, as he himself announced every time a newsman was within earshot. Which, translated, means there was a plenitude of riches; the customers got their money's worth of girls, melodies, dancing, jokes, personalities, pretty clothes, sumptuous scenery and girls. Before scoffing at this tintype from the dear dead days beyond recall, let us pause and meditate; there may be a message for us gathered here today. That is, if you have wondered why a sizable portion of the citizenry don't bestir themselves from their TV boxes, dress, brave the streets of our Land, acquire tickets to the legitimate theatre through illegitimate channels, squeeze into a musty emporium, stare at some bentwood chairs lined up on a platform, and finally get shouted at by indeterminate gypsies in raunchy leotards. We cannot turn back the clock, to coin a phrase; we have grown up and put aside childish things, such as the books for old musical shows, but the young designer should be prepared to furnish more than those bentwood chairs when the pendulum swings to the second coming of Magic Time. There is a spreading disenchantment with the Puritanical emptiness of the exposed platform, the exposed lights and the exposed epidermis. At least the designing fraternity can bring a spot or two of color onstage—recycled color, that is.

Ferdinando Galli-Bibiena (1657-1713) Harbor

II.
Background: Craig, Appia, Etc.

The pageant of scenic investiture down through recorded time is not our province. It is not that others have Page references for illustrations covered it once and for all (see "Staging & Stage Design" by scholar H. Bay, *Encyclopaedia Britannica III*), but because the contemporary theatre in its exorbitantly eclectic way exhibits in tabloid form all the variations of scenic art. That certain styles are but empty, decorative shells of what were once vital world views is of interest only when we recognize those styles for what they are today—empty, decorative shells. It is neither profitable, nor possible for that matter, to project ourselves into the conceptual frames of distant historical epochs.

Let us chart a fast survey of twentieth-century trends in Decor that in the telling will expose the rock-bottom ingredients of standard dramatic design.

Naturalism, which dominates the acting profession to this very day, was questioned in theatrical decor at 16 the turn of the century. The manner in which a thespian flicks a cigarette while gracefully draped over a mantelpiece (or scratching his T-shirt) is a small, transient piece of business, but the endless accumulation of kitchen sinks, portieres and bric-a-brac becomes oppressively obtrusive and ultimately pointless. Once the novelty of replacing flappy canvas with 3-D modeling wore off, the brainy stage artisans concluded that so much real stuff uncritically dumped on the stage was just as deceptive as paint and as irrelevant to the

Roman encampment   (Czechoslovakia, 1767)

17 higher purposes of the drama. The Symbolists led the way by clearing out the clutter and planting one or two mood-laden shapes in a vague surround. Those were the gay times of the Theatre Unfettered, with Edward Gordon Craig piping the children into the Never Never Land of mist, bombast and all-purpose screens. Lately it is fashionable to upgrade Craig for his inspirational words, but they have nothing to say to 18 us. In Moscow Meyerhold was stripping off all the trimmings right down to the unabashed platform and the exercise bars for acrobats; in Berlin Jessner was piling up those steps that to this day make American university stages indistinguishable from lumber yards; Wagner's Bayreuth was busying up the prototype of 19, 20 Hitler's pageants; Germanic machinery was getting out of hand with vast plaster domes, turntables and elevators; the art of sculpture replaced the art of painting on the shaky theory that an abstract solid was closer to Eternal Truth than two-dimensional brushwork; distorted, toppling shapes were the proper personifications of what really went on in the lower levels of the human psyche (i.e., Expressionism). Incidentally, much has been said about Reinhardt's influence on the German Expressionist cinema but little about that cinema's influence on international stage design. [See *The Haunted Screen* by Eisner. Eisner recalls that in the last grim years of World War I a shortage of materials and money forced Reinhardt to alter his productions. He retreated to a unit set of two immense columns right and left flanking the huge 27 revolve. The Books omit mention of such lowly reasons for stylistic changes.] Universal Film A.G.'s edict that everything, interiors and exteriors, must be shot in the studio created an overpowering claustrophobic universe, "landscape imbued with soul," that stamped its intense subjectivity on a generation of scenic

Ciceri "*Gustave III*" *(Rome, 1833)*

designers. Mephisto offered a world brought into being by the audience's own dramatic imagination. The 21, 23
International Theatre Exposition in New York in 1926 brought Kaiser's *Gas*, Toller's *Transfiguration* and 24, 28
Man and the Masses as well as works by Meyerhold and Barlach. This is the exhibit that hung America's 29
try at Expressionism: Jones's *Skyscraper*, Oenslager's *Pinwheel*, Gorelik's *King Hunger* and *R.U.R.*, and
Throckmorton's O'Neill designs. Initiated, of course, by Reinhardt, primitive and Oriental cultures were
lightly dipped into for exotica. The ol' debbil proscenium arch came in for a tongue-lashing. All in all,
scenic renovations would resurrect the moribund theatre from its sloth of bourgeois peccadilloes and
frumpy furnishings.

    The reverberations of the New Stagecraft that reached our shores were softer and far less overwhelming
than those breathless books indicate. The bulk of the product filling our commercial playhouses was still
surrounded with acres of meticulously painted literal detail, either on inflated interior box sets or on the

old-time wings, borders and blackcloths. The hallowed procedure was for the director (who might also be

30, 31 the actor-manager) to dispatch a ground plan to the scenic shop, where an employee dreamed up a colored

model on top of the ground plan. A minimum of thought was given to mood, atmosphere and those

32 qualities peculiar to the script, and maximum attention was paid to such generalities as period architectural fidelity. This is not surprising, since the playscript and what transpired at rehearsals was not considered the business of the mere vendor of pictorial ornament, the scenic studio. Scenic artists haunted the museums and the galleries but seldom attended the legitimate theatre. The manufactured drops—Versailles Gardens, City Street, Elegant Drawing Room with Center Door Fancy—ordered by number from the catalog didn't die out until the Depression and the films finally did in Vaudeville and the Road. The richest store of this mail-order scenery is at Ohio State, where sketches, models and even some drops were acquired from the Armbuster Studios that, operating out of Columbus, furnished backgrounds for reps, acts, minstrel and Toby shows playing the Midwest.

The New Day dawned rather quietly on the fringes of the commercial theatre. In the bosom of experimental groups, a newcomer, the designer, came into being. For the first time in the American theatre a scenic artist was *in* the theatre at the birth of a production. He was an equal partner of the author, the director and the producer in planning the overall shape of the staging. As these groups flourished and expanded and finally invaded Broadway, the designer tagged along. He started picking up commissions from the more artistic established managers, such as Arthur Hopkins and Winthrop Ames. By the late '20s the designers had won the critical dominance of our theatre, but statistically the majority of offerings were still backed up with the stuff ground out by the studios. Not until the World War II boom were most plays mounted with the stamp of the individual designer upon them.

A subdued and tasteful realism was the general style permeating American scenic design and still is,

33, 34 although five decades have come and gone. Through the years the constant motif has been an artist's poetic

35, 36 image of the theme of a dramatic work—a unique, created, total environment. The surroundings, furnishings and needed properties are filtered through the screen of the designer's artistic choice and the distilled

37, 38 essence synthesized into a visual statement of the spirit of the play. This appears to be a fair definition of the function of all scenery; similar formulations abound in the writings on modern stagecraft. Actually it represents a limited outlook, one that is confined within the Faustian concept, the priority of the individual soul: the self-contained aesthetic world onstage indebted to the world out there only for the raw material it has taken and transmitted into a shimmering vision.

"... a stage craft which found its first principles in the synthetic ideal: imaginative invention, contributive expressiveness, atmospheric beauty, subordination of specific interest to creation of mood."—Sheldon Cheney, *The Art Theatre*, 1917.

The Romantic setting exudes symbolic connotations, a stylistic individuality and an exquisite simplicity. The premium attached to these select virtues flows out of the philosophic matrix of the idealistic hero confronting an alien world. The hermetically closed setting is the extension of the protagonist's sensibility. It is isolated in a void by the magic of the lighting; nothing from mundane actuality must intrude. Its fullest expression, fulfilling the words of the soothsayers Craig and Appia, is the late Wieland Wagner's staging in

39 the temple at Bayreuth. Beings float on an island surrounded by the primal elements in constant flux (the

14

Gates & Morange Studios   "Daughter of Heaven"   (New York, 1914)

"Erdgeist" (Kleines Theater, 1902)

elements courtesy of three million dollars' worth of projection equipment from the German electrical trust).

Page references for illustrations

40   Our home-grown product has not been so pure since the pioneer splurge of Jones and Geddes—and Geddes became more fascinated with grand engineering than poetics.

41   Lee Simonson was the vocal advocate of a more rational, subdued product—practical carpentry that was sensibly attuned to the majority of Broadway attractions and their fussing over petty personal doings. This diluted version of high-flown fancy was labeled "selective realism." It was not a happy phrase. Any artistic endeavor is selective, and the realism part was downright misleading. Realism connotes more than fidelity to surface naturalism; it builds on a recognition of the primacy of social forces and respects the claims of history. Hardly a proper description for scenery that for all its incorporation of literal scraps is just as idealistic and wedded to illusionism as the out-and-out poetic numbers. We are talking about the main line of scenic design in America, up to and including today. Within this constant of pictorial-psychological stagecraft there have been minor shifts of emphasis. The early '30s saw a skittering away from the sledgehammer symbolism of the arty, flamboyant '20s and the settling down with built units, trim, molding

and exquisite appurtenances. Research took on the dignity of Scripture. The Designer's Coloring Book seemed to be the Measured Drawings of the American Wing of the Metropolitan Museum. George Jean Nathan tagged this decor Beekman Place refinement; the English designer Kenneth Rowall attributes it to 42, 43 the wand of the Wicked Fairy, Good Taste. As building grew more cumbersome, revolvers, jackknives, sliding stages and wagons proliferated.

Along about the beginning of the '40s, dramatists started breaking up the three-act format into linear strands of short episodes, the scenic designers devised montage on wheels for whisking about sharply drawn fragments—shorthand indications of locale. Gauzes imported from musicals softened the segues between scenes, and before long the toothpick skeletons supplanted the pieces of three-dimensional architecture that had posed the problem of where and how to slur the edges of the too-solid hunks. The open skeleton frame was a great assist to the simultaneous scenes spread across the stage (interior-exterior, multiple rooms, upstairs-downstairs, etc.). The craze for gauze cum toothpick skeletons ruled the '50s and was deemed the only Genuine, Official type of "Imaginative" Scenery—the only correct form of chic decor.

For special occasions the skeletons tended to be scrawny and characterless: Shakespeare and other classics cry out for massive carved blocks, Stonehenge fashion, dark reminders of primitive kingdoms and 44, 45 the elemental condition of mankind. Under the weight of the machines and with Nature shriveling away, 46 the '60s were haunted by visions of dim and distant epochs when life *must* have had shape and grandeur and meaning. Even the contemporary interior for Pinter's *Homecoming* is really a vast, creepy, archaic tomb, mysteriously preserved on a back street in Londontown.

An aside: Something got mislaid in the switchover from the solid boxes to the skeletons and distressed masonry—that something is the emotionally charged environment totally hemming in fictional characters. 47, 48 The intelligence and sensitivity devoted to creating dramatically appropriate living space were lavished on 49, 50 every minute detail of the enclosed cube. When fourth-wall thinking became passe and the ceiling and the walls were sensibly discarded, attention to the psychological rightness of the remaining items also vanished—a preoccupation with the artistic delicacy of framework that too often is interchangeable from

Adolphe Appia
"Das Rheingold"
(Basel, 1923)

Antonin Heythum
(Prague, 1920)

Page
references
for
illustrations

show to show. No one would campaign to sneak the ceilings back, but attention must be paid to the dramatic truth and the unique flavor of the remaining objects that form the home of the stage characters.

Smack in the middle of the Romantic Tradition, and proud of it, is American musical comedy design. Because the musical theatre is touted as America's contribution to world theatre, the scenic embellishments for same in their slaphappy way have added a little elan to our daily rounds. Words and pictures are paltry approximations of any live show, but in struggling to impart the flavor of the settings for bygone musicals, well. . . . Anyway, the fussy spreads of foliage, architectural ornament and endless vistas that blocked out the backwalls of our nation's playhouses were finally junked when Joseph Urban arrived from Vienna complete with a studio's worth of scenic painters and draftsmen and introduced the patterned simplicity of the Austrian Secessionist movement—pretty daring trimmings for World War I opera-goers. Urban tied up with Ziegfeld, and a lush Graustark backed up the ladies of the ensemble. Flat canvas lost out to shimmering plush and glittering appliqué on nets and heady rich skies— a feast for the eyes, you might say. Lost around the edges of the Urban epoch were many greasepaint cousins of Klimt, Moreau, and Lepape; notably John Wenger.

51, 52

53, 54

18

Wilhelm Reinking   "Aida"   (Hamburg, 1939)

When the very clever revues breezed in around 1930 something lighter and sharper was called for, and a brash young fellow of nineteen, Albert Johnson, took over. Overnight his dashed-off Raoul Dufys with their swaths of perky color and the dancing calligraphic line became the one and only style acceptable for live shows with music. Vincent Minelli and Raoul Pene du Bois continued the lighthearted carnival. Not until well into World War II did the second-hand Dufys fade out with the death of the smarty revues. The period book show crossed with the Dance Moderne became the rage, the sweet Valentines to the America

Caspar Neher   "Macbeth"   (Hamburg, 1942)

Boris Aronson "Tenth Commandment" *[model] (New York, 1926)*

Page references for illustrations

56   that never was. The embroidered, painty, frou-frou drops and cut-outs initiated by Lemuel Ayres for *Oklahoma* and *Bloomer Girl,* and myself for *Up in Central Park,* continued through Oliver Smith's *High Button Shoes,* my *Showboat* and was finally wrapped up with *Music Man.* Wringing nostalgia out of

57, 58   gingerbread fretwork, flouncy curtains and amusement-park ornament was good, clean fun. Ah, yes sir, *that* was Escape.

59   Along with the starched crinolines, came the big spenders to squire the overblown musicals. The more extravagantly inflated the physical production the juicier, as size could hide the thievery.

      After the World War II splurge leveled off a certain—I guess the word is sophistication—smoothed out the scenery; everything was lighter and more brittle. The open change in front of the audience's very eyes became the norm. The plush hangings and the vicarious bordellos were gone and the smart window displays and borrowings from the graphic arts were in. The forerunner was Oliver Smith's *On The Town.* At best it

62 was a tart mint frappe; at worst, year before last's *Harper's Bazaar.* Lately more weight has been thrown on

61 projections, on mechanization and on some variant of a unit structure. Of the recent batch of designers

63, 64 only Ming Cho Lee has not been content with minor stylistic deviations. His elegant constructions have

60, 65 made a definite personal statement. A franker treatment of stage space has pretty much wiped out the succession of full stage pictures, and that is about where we are in the decorating of Broadway with music.

      The American Musical Theatre, Macmillan for C.B.S., has the aura of an institutional prestige book, but Lehman Engel's experience as a musical director makes for the clearest story in print of how musicals are assembled.

      Fine art, as in easel painting, has impinged on the Broadway product indirectly via design for ballet and opera. The finicky vistas from LaScala, Covent Garden and the Paris Opera gave way to the gorgeous vistas of the Russians: Bakst, Golovin, Anisfeld, Benois, Gontcharova, Larionov and Doboujinsky. Diaghilev's Ballet Russe not only imported these purple temperaments into the Western World, but also distributed commissions to the entire pantheon of Post-Impressionist painters. There is an extensive library of the memoirs of everyone within knife-throwing distance of the Ballet Russe, but the flavorsome writing is one chapter in Philippe Jullian's *Prince of Aesthetes: Count Robert de Montesquiou.* The exhaustive treatise is *Diaghilev* by Boris Kochno. Easel painting and theatre is not a marriage made in heaven. Through galleries and reproductions we receive a biased account of art onstage. The more perfect the picture, by the canons of line, form and color, the greater the likelihood that its self-contained composition will war with the small actors, dancers and singers perspiring in front of its pictorial glory. "Art lovers can never understand why all stage designing isn't done by 'great' painters and sculptors. What is necessary, however, is an incomplete design; a design that has clarity without rigidity; one that could be called 'open' as against 'shut.' This is the essence of theatrical thinking: a true theatre designer will think of his designs as being all the time in motion, in action in relation to what the actor brings to a scene as it unfolds. In other words, unlike the easel painter, in two dimensions, or the sculptor in three, the designer thinks in terms of the fourth dimension, the passage of time—not the stage picture, but the stage moving picture."—Peter Brook, *The Empty Space.* Matisse, Leger, Gris, Braque and other giants of the atelier who decorated the ballet are handy object lessons. Picasso, a ham actor and amazingly adaptive to different media, was an exception.

66, 67 The looser illustrators have fared better behind the footlights. Berman, Berard, Tchelitchew, Piper, Whistler,

Donald Oenslager   "Pinwheel"   (New York, 1927)

Rouben Ter-Arutunian "*Seven Deadly Sins*" *(New York, 1958)*

Page
references
for
Illustrations

Hurry, Bailey, all embellished the ballet and occasionally helped the lagging opera. Although pre-1946, 68, 69
George Amberg's *Art in Modern Ballet* contains a lucid, still vital text that separates the relevant and 70, 71
irrelevant gifts that painters bestow upon the theatre. 72

And that brings us to a heavy picture book, *Art and the Stage in the 20th Century.* Very fancy, very impressive and very irritating. It disdains to acknowledge that anyone might have the effrontery to question its premise that only Fine Artists are worthy of dreaming up Backgrounds for the Stage—and backgrounds is the precise word. Designers are mere tradesmen and as such beneath contempt, pedestrians worrying about such details as what the dramatic event is about . . . imagine? No sensitivity to the Plastic Organization of Space. Being one of the on-foot humanoids I cannot see anything so marvelous about a Leger too big to fit into a frame on a wall. For instance, on Brecht's designer Neher: "Fundamentally he is not carrying out a work of creation but a work of arrangement. It takes its guidelines from the dramatic structure of the play . . . . " Obviously a menial approach in contradistinction to so many Real Artists illustrated in the book, who after tearful pleas from the Ballet Russe posted a sketch or two lying around the studio, washing their hands of the messy business of overseeing peasants translate their creations into big hanging things at the back of the stage.

The large and expensive volume reveals a few nuggets. Here is a quote from the great Leon Bakst, "The first tendency, which I call 'Protestant,' takes as its point of departure renunciation of beautiful, sumptuous, and dominant decor, claiming that such settings impede full apprehension of the word. It is exactly as if a believing Protestant faced with the cathedral of Notre Dame were to complain that the beauty and splendor of this magnificent but religious architecture made it impossible for him to concentrate on the word of God . . . . This is a negative aesthetic born of fear . . . . The theory of Gordon Craig . . . a mediocre stage designer but an eloquent speaker—owes its whole success to this negative aesthetic, which, incidentally, has the advantage of being rather economical. In discussions the English never forget to bring up this argument in support of their paradoxical Craig. Furthermore, this 'Protestant' gentleman fosters the unhealthy tendency to make all settings the same; for his economical basic elements (neutral curtains, indications of walls, conventional steps) do not spring from the living particularly of this play or that, but from a *formula* that can be applied to any works of art whatever and will finally lead to a monotony that in the long run will produce irritation. I, in any case, cannot distinguish these 'Protestant' decors from one another, whether they are the sets for *Hamlet* in New York, a Maeterlinck in Paris, or a Bernard Shaw in London. A curtain on the right, a wall on the left, a so-called 'gigantic' column in the background, in the center 'steps' (why?). . . . Change them around a little and you could perform the second act against them, or a different play altogether. The effect remains the same. Poverty, monotony . . . . "

Opera is opera, and one is tempted to let it go at that; so little has changed since the first elephants lumbered through the first *Aida* processional. After a while one gets the eerie sensation that all the Gorgeous Trappings for opera and ballet add up to a continuous showing of *The Tales of Hoffmann* catered 73 by Rumpelmayer's. The machinery to move even heftier-built sets becomes more elaborate with each passing day.

The only glimmering of a better tomorrow is Feldenstein and his East Berlin Opera. Much has been written expounding his theories, but they are quite simple: Stars if they wish to participate must act with everyone else and fit into a *dramatic* ensemble in which music takes a sizable but not overwhelming position. That isn't all, the startling innovation is that the characters listed in the libretto must be

74, 75 transformed into human beings who have reasons for opening their mouths. The endless preparation time, attention to detail and interminable technical rehearsals assure truly cohesive productions—and the envy of the rest of the world. (Isn't it sad that one must propagandize for a Realistic Lyric Theatre!)

76, 77 As traditional opera crumbles away, up-to-date visual wrappings disguise the downward journey; but it is
78, 79 a stopgap, a holding action. True lyric theatre on the lines of Feldenstein's precepts is not around the corner, however, because in addition to completely fresh thinking, it requires large subsidies and long-term ensembles. A tilting revolving stage will not solve the dilemma of our most sumptuous anachronism.

80, 81 Back in our gaudy hometown opry house let us call upon a designer who has consistently brought some
82 loveliness to this form. We give you Robert O'Hearn: "So how do you design an opera? I don't really know. You can approach it from many angles—research, color, style—but suddenly a small pencil scribble becomes something in a way often mysterious even to the designer himself, and that is the most thrilling and inexplicable moment. All the rest is preparing for that moment and then cherishing it, developing and carrying it through.... For *Die Frau Ohne Schatten* I took my basic patterns not from artistic or anthropological or historical research, but from minute living organisms. The great patterns on stage are abstracted from enlarged photographs of natural phenomena. A microscope photograph of a frog's eye is the basis of one. Another is based on photographs of the crystalline structure of quartz...."

From the grand technical juggernauts of the grand opera houses of Central Europe comes much advanced work in projected scenery, but we shall examine this under lighting.

At this writing two internationally recognized scenic artists, the Englishman Sean Kenny and the Czech
83, 84 Joseph Svoboda, merit attention. Kenny, a latter-day Normal Bel Geddes, who died at the age of forty was bursting with underwater cities, streamlined knockdown amphitheatres and gigantic toys that did marvelous tricks—it was circus time in outer space. Svoboda is a sizable phenomenon. After 350 productions in Europe and design leadership of the Prague National Theatre he hit America with a blockbuster, the Czech Pavilion at Montreal Expo '67—and threw in a sideshow in the amusement area, Laterna Magika. The orchestrated bombardment of films and stills—projecting, receding, expanding, contracting—and cascading over fluctuating surfaces and spectators alike—was the most overpowering kinetic assault in the memory of man. From theatrical gatherings, through movie-makers, to Madison Avenue the reaction was loud and instantaneous: multi-screen dynamic images are the thing. Svoboda's architectural-mechanical predilections feature moving blocks, projections and mirrors; the spine of his theory is that all scenic elements must appear and disappear, shift and flow, rhythmically complement the development of the drama (see Jarka Burian's *The Scenography of Josef Svoboda*). It is unfair to judge his staggering and varied output by our limited exposure to his Czech-industry sales pitch and the pretentious vulgarity of the *Tales of Hoffmann* on Laterna Magika. The static pictorial statement planted on stage is definitely headed for the dustbin, and so far the exploitation of science behind the footlights is embarrassingly minuscule, but the key question is this: Is the film plus mechanization of the stage the future or is it the last fascinating

Otto Hunter & Erich Kettlehut "Siegfried" [film] (1924)

plaything of a dying theatre? Is it The Stagecraft In The Age of Science or is it out-of-sight packaging for Page references for illustrations old dramaturgy and new detergents? I am suspicious of a preoccupation with mechanics bordering on fetishism. It distracts from the deep examination of human activity, which is the business of theatrics. My bias files the electronic marvels right here in the historical background slot rather than as the thrilling curtain.

84, 85
86, 87

88
Lately the pictorialist-illusionist setting of the last one hundred years isn't automatically accepted as the one and only way to fill up the stage. Providing a unified, closed environment tailored to the theme, mood and atmosphere of the psychological drama is a special viewpoint peculiar to the historically constricted dramaturgy it complements. We shall quote from the prophet Brecht (Frederich Ewen, *Bertolt Brecht*):

"The bourgeois theatre emphasizes the timelessness of its objects. Its representation of people is bound by the alleged 'eternally human'. Its story is arranged in such a way as to create 'universal' situations that

Mordecai Gorelik   "King Hunger"   (1924)

28

Ernst Stern "Lysistrata" (Berlin, 1908)

allow Man with a capital M to express himself of every period and every color. All its incidents are just one enormous cue, and this cue is followed by the 'eternal' response. . . . The cue can take account of what is special, different; the response is shared, there is no element of difference in it. This notion may allow that such a thing as history exists, but it is nonetheless unhistorical. A few circumstances vary, the environments are altered, but Man remains unchanged. History applies to the environment, not to Man. The environment is remarkably unimportant, is treated simply as a pretext; it is a variable quality and something remarkably inhuman; it exists in fact apart from Man, confronts him as a coherent whole, whereas he is a fixed quantity, eternally unchanged. The idea of man as a function of the environment and the environment as a function of man, i.e., the breaking up of the environment into relationships between men, corresponds to a new way of thinking, the historical way. . . .

"When the epic theatre's methods penetrate the opera the first result is a radical separation of the elements. The great struggle for supremacy between words, music and production—which always brings up the question 'which is the pretext for what?' is the music the pretext for the events on the stage, or are these the pretext for the music? etc.—can simply be by-passed by radically separating the elements. So long as the expression 'integrated work of art' means that the integration is a muddle, so long as the arts are supposed to be 'fused' together, each will act as the merest 'feed' to the rest. The process of fusion extends to the spectator, who gets thrown into the melting pot too and becomes a passive (suffering) part of the total work of art. Witchcraft of this sort must of course be fought against. . . .

"In his designs he provides no 'decor,' frames and backgrounds, but constructs space for 'people' to experience something. . . . It's more important nowadays for the set to tell the spectator he's in a theatre than to tell him he's in, say, Aulis. The theatre must acquire the same fascinating reality as a sporting arena during a boxing match. . . . If a set represents a town it must look like a town that has been built to last precisely two hours. One must conjure up the reality of time."

Gates & Morange Studios Model room   (1912)

Gates & Morange Studios Advertising drop (New York, 1912)

All these words of wisdom have led the literal-minded to construct boxing rings and expose the brick walls of theatres. Most American mountings of Brecht appear to be the handiwork of a serious eunuch laboring within a very modest budget.

There is a worldwide rash of neo-Brechtian staging, the classics having been the hardest hit. Perhaps neo-Brechtian is too sunny a title for the lumpen desecration of the master's precepts; let's tag it Incinerator Neolithic. Protocol decrees tortured burlap, mutilated animal pelts, corroded metal, clunky ornaments pillaged from the burial mounds of the Vikings; all hung together with distressed thongs, then blow-torched. The coup de grâce is a patina of soot administered by Torquemada's helpers. The charcoal ensemble is relieved by a gay glint of burnt coffee under the doomsday glare of the white operating lights. I have toyed with a theory that all the casts of these entertainments are nothing but the original crew who

Armbuster Studios Asbestos curtain (c. 1900)

swarmed around the base of Notre Dame, vainly clutching at Lon Chaney. I will be vindicated by excavation of the Universal backlot—they are all there, chained in caves between engagements.

Page references • for illustration

89 Pre-Brecht presentational staging, the "theatre theatrical," originated with Constructivism in the new Soviet Union. Stripping off the ornamented encrustations of the ancient regime, they planted naked apparatus on the naked platform. Piscator in pre-Hitler Germany elaborated this base with what we now call multi-media. Flaying around for violent weapons to shake up his audiences he piled up treadmills, cartoons, film and involved moving structures.

89 The American extension was the Living Newspaper division of Federal Theatre in the mid-'30s. Assembled newspaper fashion, the different editions, each built around a single public issue, seized on any handy device to project the content: a loudspeaker character, a Little Man protagonist, burlesque bits, film clips, cartoon slides, puppets, ventriloquists, masks, kindergarten games, patter songs, etc. Although my

Herman Rosse "The Great Magoo" (New York, 1932)

giant composite tenement for *one third of a nation* looms large in the memory album, it is more profitable to study the script for *Power (Federal Theatre Plays)* to discover how just the right, sharp gimmick was found to dramatize the facts concretely. The Living Newspaper spawned a brood of pale children—You Are There as Time Marches On, Up the Monongahela and Down the Housatonic with Just Plain Folks. Not only was the bite of the original missing, but a slothful dependence on commentary, plus statistics, plus pictures overlooked Living News editor Arthur Arent's ingenuity in fastening onto the exact theatricalization for each segment of the dry raw material. The aridity of today's Fact Theatre stems from this antiseptic nicety—the artistic snobbery that distains to purloin lively bits from our comic treasury, advertising or just junk lying around the streets of our fair cities. But enough of that until we confront the New Theatre. Let us pass on to the perilous journey from drawing board to the bewitching night when Life and Death await the Word from a journalist in the pay of the *New York Times.*

Herman Rosse   "The Great Magoo"   (New York, 1932)

Donald Oenslager   "Fabulous Invalid"   (New York, 1938)

Donald Oenslager "Fabulous Invalid" *(New York, 1938)*

Boris Aronson   "Gentle People"   (New York, 1939)

Lemuel Ayres "The Pirate" (New York, 1942)

Jo Mielziner "Look Homeward, Angel" (New York, 1957)

Ming Cho Lee   "Gnadiges-Fraulein"   [model]   (New York, 1966)

Wieland Wagner "Parsifal" (Beyreuth, 1955)

Robert Edmond Jones   "Camille"   (Central City, 1932)

Norman Bel Geddes "The Patriot" (New York, 1928)

Lee Simonson   "Jane Eyre" (New York, 1936)

Rex Whistler "An Ideal Husband" (London, 1943)

Howard Bay "Deep Are the Roots" (New York, 1945)

Donald Oenslager   "The Leading Lady"   (New York, 1948)

Howard Bay   "Toys in the Attic"   (New York, 1960)

Emil Siki "Hamlet" (Budapest, 1962)

Emil Siki "Hamlet" (Budapest, 1962)

Ming Cho Lee   "Richard III"   (New York, 1966)

Ralph Koltai   "Back to Methuselah"   (London, 1969)

William Mickley   "The Devils"   (Brandeis University, 1970)

46

Howard Bay "*Brooklyn, U.S.A.*" *(New York, 1941)*

George Wakevitch   "Sud"   (Paris, 1953)

Ming Cho Lee   "Peer Gynt" (New York, 1969)

Howard Bay   "Peer Gynt"   (1939)

Joseph Urban "Garden of Paradise" (New York, 1914)

Joseph Urban   "Garden of Paradise"   (New York, 1914)

Joseph Urban   "Garden of Paradise"   (New York, 1914)

John Wenger *"Romance"* *(New York, 1921)*

John Wenger "Indian Love Lyrics" (New York, 1922)

54

Albert Johnson   "As Thousands Cheer"   (New York, 1933)

Albert Johnson   "As Thousands Cheer"   (New York, 1933)

Lemuel Ayres   "Bloomer Girl"   (New York, 1944)

Howard Bay   "Up in Central Park"   (New York, 1945)

Howard Bay   "Music Man"   (New York, 1957)

Howard Bay *"Show Boat"* *(New York, 1954)*

Harry Horner   "Star and Garter"   (New York, 1942)

Howard Bay   "Follow the Girls"   (New York, 1941)

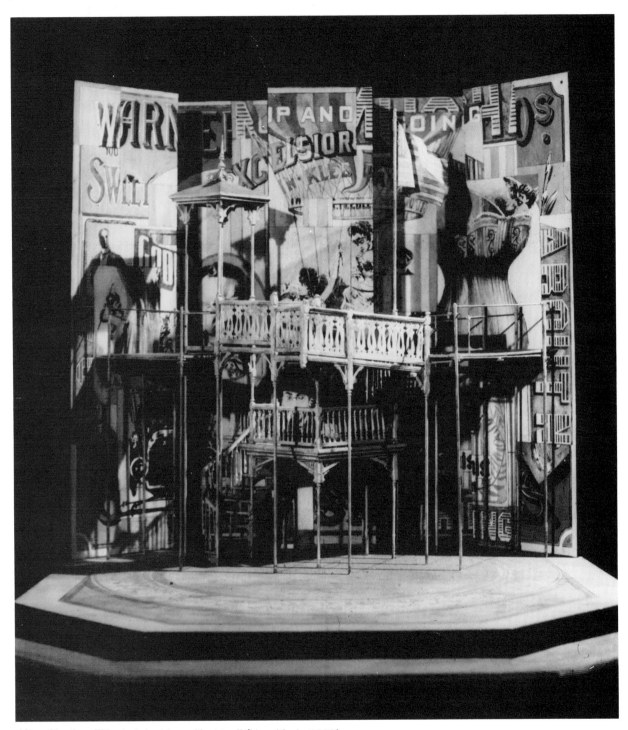

Ming Cho Lee ''Much Ado About Nothing'' (New York, 1968)

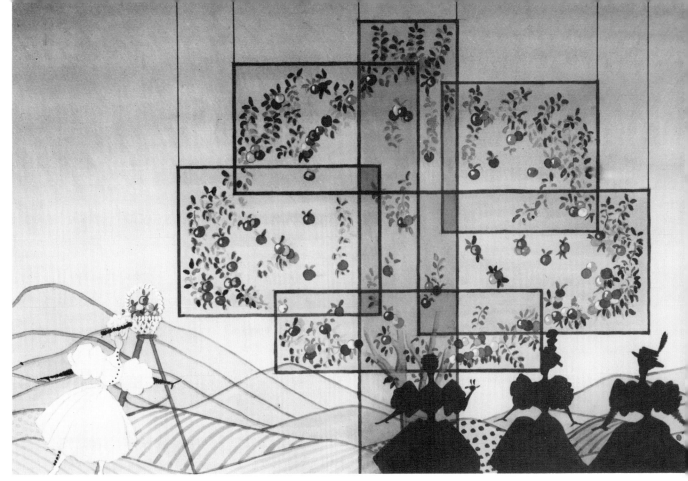

William Eckart & Jean Eckart   "The Golden Apple"   (New York, 1954)

William Eckart & Jean Eckart   "Mame"   (New York, 1966)

Oliver Smith   "On the Town"   (New York, 1944)

Jo Mielziner "1776" (New York, 1969)

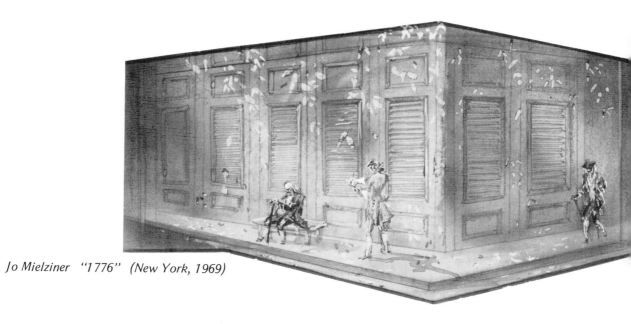

Jo Mielziner "1776" (New York, 1969)

Boris Aronson "Company" (New York, 1970)

Ming Cho Lee "Faust" (New York, 1968)

Eugene Berman   "Rigoletto"   (New York, 1951)

Christian Berard   "Madwoman of Chaillot"
(Paris, 1945)

John Piper   "Turn of the Screw"   (London, 1954)

Rouben Ter-Arutunian   "Swan Lake"   (New York, 1962)

Rouben Ter-Arutunian   "Pallaeus & Melisande"   (Spoleto, 1966)

Donald Oenslager "The Ballad of Baby Doe" (Central City, 1956)

Howard Bay   "Carmen"   (San Francisco, 1959)

Tichy   "Petrushka"   (Prague, 1948)

Howard Bay   "Magdalena"   (Los Angeles, 1948)

Metropolitan Opera Revolving Stage

Rudolph Heinrich   "Magic Flute"   (East Berlin, 1954/60)

Reinhart Zimmermann   "Beggar's Opera"
(East Berlin, 1963)

Reinhart Zimmermann   "Beggar's Opera"
(East Berlin, 1963)

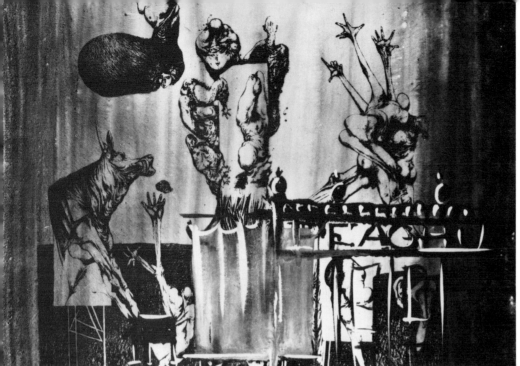

Sujan   "Threepenny Opera"
(Bratislava, 1966)

Rudolph Heinrich   "Parsifal"
(Hamburg, 1967)

Vychodil   "Thief-woman from London" (Prague, 1962)

John Bury   "Moses and Aaron" (London)

77

Boris Aronson "Fidelio" (New York, 1970)

Boris Aronson "Fidelio" (New York, 1970)

Robert O'Hearn "Die Frau ohne Schatten" (New York, 1966)

Robert O'Hearn "Die Frau ohne Schatten" (New York, 1966)

Metropolitan Opera House Backstage Three Sets: Upstairs, Onstage and Upstage

Sean Kenny "Blitz" (London, 1962)

Sean Kenny "Blitz" (London, 1962)

*Josef Svoboda "August Sunday"
(Prague, 1958)*

*Teo Otto "The Devil and the
Good Lord" (Zurich, 1952)*

84

V. Mahenic   "Master Hanus"   (Belgrade, 1965)

Vychodil "The White Illness" (Bratislava, 1958)

Rene Allio "Dead Souls" (Lyon, 1960)

Koltai   "Resurrection"
(Prague, 1962)

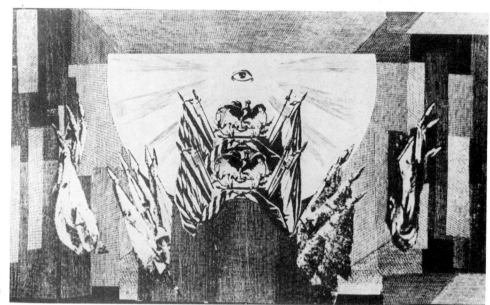

Hans-Ulrich Schmuckle
"Robespierre" (Berlin, 1963)

Howard Bay
"one third of a nation"
(New York, 1938)

III.
The Designer & The Production Process

It is a puzzlement to decide which path to take in explaining the designer's role in the production process. I have opted for the straight line from script to opening night, knowing that the weakness of this neat journey is that it postpones backstage orientation until the assembly of the show. Unquestionably, there are no grounds for deeming yourself even a potential artist of stage effects unless you've had more than a cursory brush with backstage. I will go further, there must be an affection bordering on passion for the very dust and medieval trappings of those quaint caverns behind asbestos curtains.

One of the smaller tragedies is the design student weaned on electronic switchboards, hydraulic lifts and mechanized grids who is lost when he bumps into the primitive fixings of Broadway and road proscenium houses. This loony, backward scene can be righted by haunting stage doors during load-ins and plugging away at humble questions addressed to the production crews of the attractions. Questions, mind you, not snooty remarks, such as: "How do you abide those beat-up, anachronistic piano boards? We banked thirty-six presets back at Central State." For a cram course in the systematic exploitation of stage space there is no substitute for watching the pros put together, run and take down a show. Beyond the information stored up from covering a variety of works in progress is the feeling for scale and proportion

Peter Rice   "Ariadne in Naxos"   (London, 1961)

that only being in the midst of the jigsaw units can give. There is another, rather mystical-sounding quality, I'm afraid—sensed from the stage side only—the stance of the set confronting the audience.

The production sequence takes off from a more or less finished script. (General laughter.) There is a way to read a play and Speedreading is not it. The first reading is all-important, an encounter never to be recaptured. One must erase from consciousness all wise backstage baggage and confront the script with a superficial version of what the old Zen characters called an Empty Mind. It must be a passive, noncritical absorption—don't fight the author's seductive attack. A seemingly aimless spell of gestation ends when the scowls of the calendar can no longer be avoided.

Labor begins on the second reading with notetaking and rough diagrams. For these preliminary jottings art materials are minimal: an automatic pencil with soft, thin, long leads; a Pink Pearl eraser; a scale ruler with one-inch-, one-half-inch- and one-quarter-inch-to-the-foot calibrations; and a pad of tracing paper. Visualization through the ground plan is the first struggle for the beginning scenic designer. One-quarter inch to the foot is a manageable scale, and the boundaries of an average stage are laid out; thirty-six-foot proscenium opening, thirty-foot depth plus a two-foot-thick proscenium and a three-foot apron, and fifteen feet offstage right and left. All measurements are taken from the center line and the back of the proscenium. Freehand plotting to scale can proceed; we will postpone drafting for a while. Broad lines of traffic, entrances, exits, possible furniture relationships are jotted down but kept tentative and fluid. Geography is kept loose by treating the stage area as space only with notations of movements from up right to down left, up center to down center, etc. Space is cubic and not merely a two-dimensional ground plan; a shorthand system of plus and minus signs marks the elevations above and below the stage floor, which is 0'—0''. Climactic moments demand mandatory patterns, and at that point one must backtrack and adjust prior movements. There are no walls or specific architecture as yet. This choreographic diagram is only a preliminary device to anchor the large rhythms of the drama and forestall the chaos of total immersion in the details that will crowd in and sidetrack the play's main thrust.

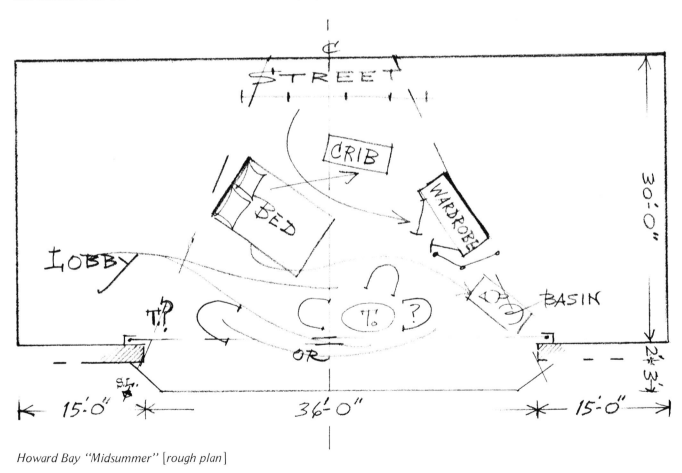

Howard Bay "Midsummer" [*rough plan*]

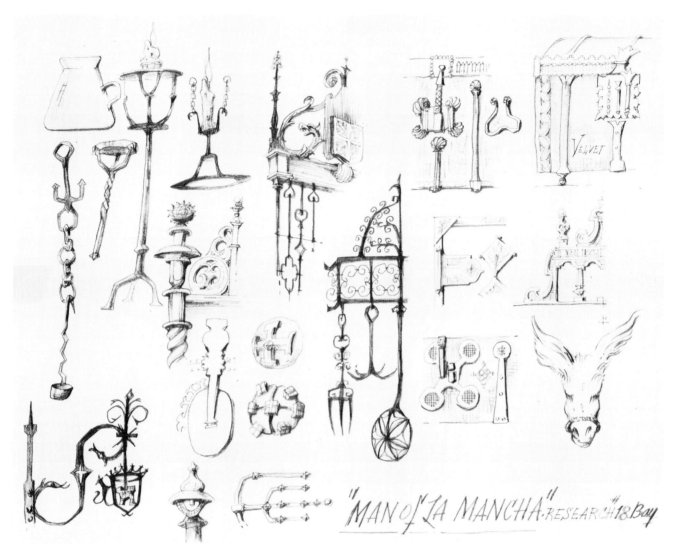

Howard Bay   "Man of La Mancha"   [research]   (New York, 1965)

This is the moment for the ancient adage that all designers are frustrated directors. This could well be true, but why? Because the process of designing dictates the quasi-director role for the designer. His initial concept must project a scheme based on key action patterns. The set is the compass for the journey of the action. The proposed format of the actors' environment is a statement of the show's direction. This plotting of the movement flow is the designer's first chore—though it surely will be revised by the director.

Next step is the research department. This step is the prime test of the well-oiled brain. The wayside is cluttered with the bleached bones of excruciatingly gifted artists who failed as practicing designers for lack of organization. Half of any research is limiting the search. Neophyte designers tend to fall into sin by heading for the Best, the Supreme Examples, the Glorious Monuments. They copy Versailles, Malmaison, San Souci, Knole and Casa d'Oro, while all the time that which lends actuality to a stage structure resides in

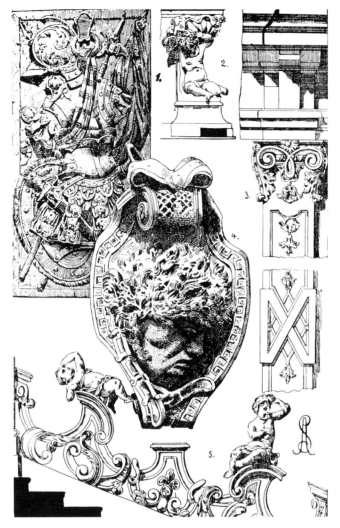

Speltz   "Styles of Ornament"   [research]

the modest daily accessories, the lived-in peculiarities of a given time and a given social layer. It takes a bit of digging, because historians seldom bother to furnish copious illustrations of the articles of ordinary existence; such stuff doesn't desecrate the eye-catching gift books. Broadway designers are indebted to the Picture Collection of the New York Public Library at 42nd Street for its mass of circulating material that covers odds and ends. The substitute, for those not within commuting distance of this repository, is the do-it-yourself morgue, a swipe file built of pictures torn out of magazines, old books and newspapers. The single, indispensable reference work is Speltz's *Styles of Ornament* (Dover paperback) which is not a bible but a springboard; the pedantry does not destroy its dense wealth. Speltz provides a quick overall period identification. The second most valuable book by virtue of its fine, detailed renderings of interiors as they

Praz "Illustrated History of Furnishings" [research]

really existed is Mario Praz's *An Illustrated History of Furnishings.* Refinements are hunted down in specialized sources—often in the corners and margins of pictures.

About tracing versus copying research: copy, because the drawing process is not automatic but forces one to sketch in the style of the research. Ceaseless sketching in the period submerges the designer in another era and renders him temporarily incapable of drawing outside that style. The trouble is that there are too many designers who sketch as if all plays were laid either in Rembrandt's Holland or in eighteenth-century Venice. If you stop to think about it, a Brooklyn tenement seldom has the look of a Gaurdi drawing that was left out in the rain any more than the cliffs of Elsinore can be brought to life by a stack of blocks hung over from a Bauhaus elementary lab course.

Howard Bay   "Tyl Ulenspiegel"

Research is a tool and a mighty indispensable tool at that. It is a step on the way that cannot be airily waved aside by dashing on to Creativity. Obviously research cannot assume the proportions of a fetish in the gluttonous Victorian scavenger-of-the-centuries manner. The designer dives into research so that everything that arrives onstage exudes the flavor of the period in a natural organic way. It must be noted that a playscript laid in, say, 1870 does not automatically mean that all the elements onstage should be circa 1870. Chances are that the building was built in 1845, that the side chairs were grandfather's, that the chest came over with the colonists—that almost everything had been accumulated over a stretch of time. The Interior Decorating Look and the scenic design approach are not of the same world. Research is chasing seemingly petty tangents in the course of assembling the collection of parts that makes any scenic ensemble right and inevitable.

On the study of art history: we have gone way beyond the Art Appreciation silliness into exhaustive, socially based courses on all sections of our visual past. That's dandy for the making of future art historians,

Michael Annals "Royal Hunt of the Sun" [roughs]

but it is not tailored for the apprentice designer who cannot devote years to cramming his noggin with the Encyclopedia of Art through the Ages. What is called for is a program labeled Research and Sources. The broad outlines of the periods would be covered but the emphasis thrown on the methods for procuring and handling source material specifically for dramatic design use. It is likely that soon much visual documentation will be available on audio-visual cassettes that plug into your TV set. A looseleaf directory of the whereabouts of material and equipment would supplement the course. In the meantime gather a file of equipment catalogs.

The ultimate sketch is the distilled essence of tiresome mounds of historical trivia. Robert Edmond Jones's designs have misled a few generations of aspiring artists because of their deceptive simplicity. The unwary beginner glances at a Jones design and sees only the skeleton of a Gothic arch. He blithely proceeds to draw the skeleton of a Gothic arch and wonders why the result appears thin and arid. The reason is that Jones first waded through a vast array of source material and then drew and drew, continually refining and purifying without losing the spirit of the original architecture. The confusing welter of history cannot be

Howard Bay "Midsummer" [sketch]

bypassed; it must be absorbed and understood—and then disregarded. The spirit will be embedded in every line. Perhaps the making of a stage designer is the last earthly use for the Beaux Arts system.

The laboriously acquired skill to render actuality without the intrusion and distortions of personal taste and mannerism is the only way to reconstruct the diversity of visual history. The galling truth is that there is no shortcut to the acquisition of drawing facility—an old-time bromide that is still fresh as a daisy as far as the scenic business is concerned. All those dusty casts, dead still lifes, Orders of Architecture, cabriole legs, and *rocaille* must be plowed through with charcoal and pencil and cramped hands and bleary eyeballs. At the end of the boring road one is equipped to put down on paper with dispatch the inspired images soaring around in the headbone. Dispatch is the key word; production schedules seldom pause for leisurely creation to flower. Ideally, the making of a designer should take off from at least two years devoted to nothing but old-fashioned atelier training in life and still life drawing and the copying of historical architectural details.

The easy paraphernalia of contemporary graphic arts, such as camerawork, overlays and diverse collage tricks, must not detour the designer from acquiring a Solid Grounding In Drawing. All these fascinating devices are exploited in the newest stagecraft, but facility with the pencil comes first. So, carry a small sketch pad in your pocket. One should constantly sketch the real world for two reasons: Sketching

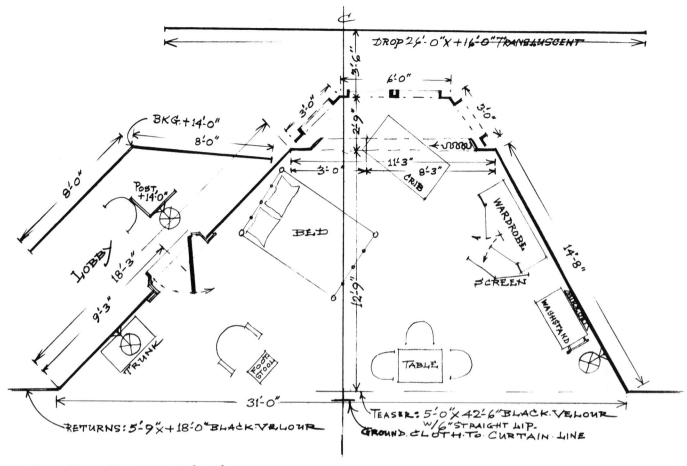

Howard Bay "Midsummer" [plan]

maintains skill as practice solidifies the techniques of the pianist. Secondly, our vision coasts along in unseeing cliché that can be broken by looking hard at everything and then literally transplanting it onto paper. Perceptual vision is not immune to historical conditioning; in fact, it is so embedded in unconscious molds that the bias of vision has only recently been noticed and scrutinized (Rudolf Arnheim, *Visual Thinking*). Forward-groping dramatists cannot be served with a static, Newtonian world built onstage.

Good old charcoal is tailored for the scenic artist due to its easy, flexible handling of light and shade. Pink Pearl and kneaded erasers can pick out highlights, and paper stumps can soften and blur edges and blend the secondary portions into ambiguous shadows. The stock progression from still life, through casts, to sketching from the model is highly recommended. Even the old, grizzled designer should persist in attending life classes to hold that fresh facility of capturing subtle flesh. The blunt softness of charcoal forces concentration on the essentials and discourages finicky embroidery of the inconsequential.

The jumble of pictorial matter, the ocular pollution, immobilizes the beginning artist. He flays around, frantically attempting to piece out a new and unique style that he can call his very own. This hectic search may pay off in the art market but it is foolish, short-term thinking for the scenic designer in the making. A hastily acquired, narrow drawing mannerism may fit one drama in scores of dramas. The rut deepens as the single style is polished and perfected while the increasing inflexibility in coping with the diverse demands of

Peter Wexler   "War and Peace"   [model]   (New York, 1964)

Peter Wexler   "War and Peace"   [roughs]   (New York, 1964)

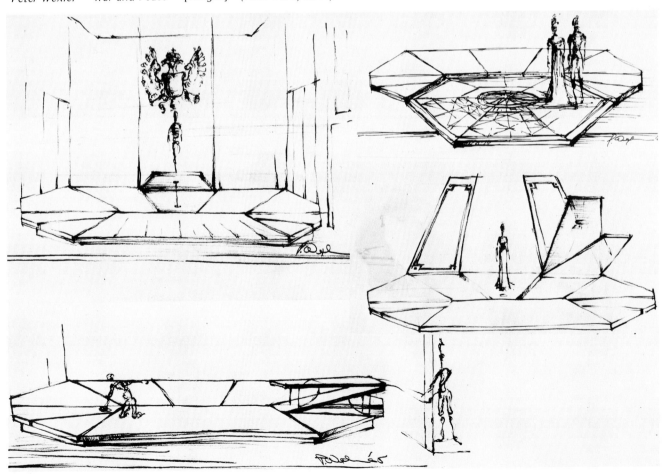

Peter Larkin   "Inherit the Wind"
(New York, 1955)

shifting theatrics isolates the designer. The proper procedure, although it seems a drag to the impatient young, is laborious acquisition of the mastery of drawing in any and all styles. One can then face the variety of the world's drama and also be alert to that which is still around the bend. A point to be made over and over again with variations is that "imagination" is not a novel surface stylization but a conceptual attack on a production. The concept slides into focus after a flock of questions are asked and answered: What is the playwright's "theme"? How does this mesh into the state of the world out there? What is the orientation of the producing outfit and their special virtues and limitations? What is the peculiar conditioning of the target audience? If a revival, why is it being revived with what new slant? How can the physical playhouse be twisted into a place unique to this event? The director comes with what talents and what failings, and how can the designer underline the former and cover up the latter? Many of these considerations seem didactic

Michael Annals   "Seagull:" Act I
(Tel Aviv, 1971)

Michael Annals "Seagull:" Act II (Tel Aviv, 1971)

Michael Annals "Seagull:" Act III (Tel Aviv, 1971)

Michael Annals "Seagull:" Act IV (Tel Aviv, 1971)

and perhaps some smell downright pretentious in dealing with the scenic fittings for a little old play on a stage. However, early thinking about where a show is going creates a trusty home base that relegates the countless details to their proper niches. Theatre is customarily put together topsy-like so cogitation and preplanning counteract the conservative meandering. As the visual whole eludes analysis by language, the final choice of specifics and the composition must remain subconscious and nonrational. Only a clear formulation of the goal of the end product will create a spine cementing the unfocalized visual data. Plainly put, the designer had better hammer out an approach early in the game because he can't later in the scurry of patching together all the technical pieces that make up the physical production.

After voluminous research and a spell of brooding, come the thumbnail sketches. At first these are wild, random little dreams unchained by all the burdensome practicalities. They are theoretically possible stabs at   97, 98 the large dimensions of the script. They may soar upward to the gridiron and push the walls outward to the alley behind and jut forward into the laps of the expensive customers. But in their crude, flamboyant way they struggle to enunciate the *raison d'être* of this one theatrical piece. They are not abstract design exercises in any line-form-color sense but a fusion of the research and the early thinking. Certain motifs continually recur, go through metamorphoses and shape up as talismen. A warning about the temptations of symbolism, which casts a spell over tender young designers. There is nothing like a cross or a swastica to lead the unwary astray. A prominent symbol is a bald, static statement not amenable to development in the course of the plot's unraveling. It just sits there in its leaden way, blocking any sensitive unfolding of the drama. Generally, the beginner tends to cram too much of the play's theme into the setting—after all there are the actors and words. The setting is the beginning, the springboard for the script, and it should not step too far beyond the audience's prejudices and preconceptions or the dramatist and the director and his cast cannot lead that audience by its collective nose into new pastures and to new conclusions.

As one's thoughts become more definite and a scheme takes shape, the original three-inch by five-inch thumbnails grow to quarter-inch scale freehand drawings. Thinking in scale takes awhile, sometimes years, so the little stick figure is always drawn in to keep things within reason. Another device helps hold inspiration to the earth: do not show stage floor but rather assume that eye level and the stage floor coincide. All elements that rest on the ground spring from the bottom line of the sketch. This method is less deceptive in depicting the ultimate size of the scenery. Rough ground plans should parallel the sketches   99 (this also helps overcome the urge to show floor in elevation sketches).

A whole subject comes up about here: namely, perspective. Even the "simplified" systems are involved, but one or another of them is unavoidable. I hesitate to recommend any single manual because different students will latch onto different presentations. You might try on for size Gwen White's *Perspective*. After diligent application to the system of your choice you can then graduate to freehand perspective with confidence.

The one-quarter-inch sketches begin to absorb more and more of the mechanical and directorial demands, modifying but not losing the concept. As detail becomes more precise, the copied research is dug out and data is lifted and incorporated. The limited gray range of the pencil and/or charcoal can be sharpened up with a black felt pen for the deep shadows and opaque white for the highlights.

A crucial decision looms up: at what point does the designer stop polishing the drawings, crawl out of seclusion and expose his ideas to the director? The deciding factor is the production schedule. A large calendar is busied up, working backward from the first public performance. Dress rehearsals and ahead of

Feliks Topolski Drawing

them technical run-throughs are penciled in, and ahead of them technical rehearsals, and ahead of them lighting, and ahead of that the load-in and set-up date. The target is the load-out—the completion of all shop execution. Depending on the workload in the shops and the shops' own estimation of time needed, that space is backed up and the date noted when working drawings are due for delivery to the shops. Calculating how much time drafting will take ahead of that period, the date is entered for director-producer approval of final designs. Now you have the segment of time remaining to design the show, which embraces not only art but the conferences and the inevitable renovations they portend. With this calendar in front of you the chances are you will grab the phone and ask for an early meeting with your director.

Obviously a director is not going to wax enthusiastic over an embryonic sketch, even if you are confident of the beauty that still resides in your cranium. A clean matte and cellophane will do wonders for a little black and white drawing. A bold, simplified ground plan should accompany same. Without duplicating the drafting section dealing with detailed working drawings, some shorthand conventions are needed for your freehand plan. First, all structural boundaries, such as proscenium, back and side walls, are marked in with heavy lines. The center and curtain lines are added, the opaque walls of the set itself drawn in solid lines,

Rex Whistler "Ballerina" (London, 1933)

openings (windows, door, arches) in dotted lines, elevations indicated with heights noted (+2'–0'', for instance) and the important furniture added in outline.

I may as well break the news right now: half of the designing business is winning friends and influencing people. At the top of the list of those to be cultivated are the directors, who come assorted—there are no prerequisites for becoming a director. A producer may decide he will try his hand and who will question the boss? In the forgotten days of the actor-managers no director was in evidence; the stage manager moved the supporting players around the stage out of the path of the star's travels. That Elmer Gantry of 44th Street, David Belasco, changed all that and firmly staked out the domain of the producer-director: the whole works. That is where we are, and it is right and proper. The director is the key; it has been discovered on several occasions that theatre is not put together by committee. The designer is number one collaborator of the director, so it behooves us to pause and examine this working relationship. Some directors are technical-minded and some are not. Many directors' reputations spring from their rewrite ability, others from their exclusive concern with and skill in the handling of actors. The technically knowledgeable ones may have fairly developed and sometimes rigid production schemes in mind before you present your

Sesshu (1420-1506)
Sumi painting

thoughts on the subject. If that happens, intelligence, flexibility and patience will be needed to blend the best possible combination of your ideas and the director's. The script has to be combed through to check all contingencies of action and business. Looking back on certain of my most successful design jobs, I am unable to separate the elements the director contributed from the ideas I dreamed up. The technically ignorant *regisseur* needs the good offices of your friendly designer well beyond the line of duty prescribed in the contract. Not only the looks of the stage but basic patterns of movement, spacing the acting area, and furniture-spotting must be hammered out and offered to the nonvisual director. Often he needs a model if the ground plan appears to him to resemble a hieroglyphic scroll. Many technically inept directors happen to be very good directors—if they have the sagacity to team up with the right designers. The dangerous one is the director with a smattering of backstage terminology who would have been a great designer if he had just taken time to learn to draw. He shines at conferences with his expansive chatter sprinkled with references to fresnels, commutators, etc. The designer is hired help, a draftsman to follow through and fill in the details of the grand plan. The only answer to this airy persiflage is to come up with an exhilarating and workable scheme and fight for it. Rhetoric and debate are not passe studies. Remember that you are the one who must turn wayward ideas into concrete, physical things that function onstage. So in the bubbly talk of staff confabs your mind must scrutinize all and sundry inspirations and race ahead to the execution problems. Your role is not that of an empirical wet blanket but that of a creative unifier who can pounce on the valuable bits and pieces and put them together. Unanimity among the working heads in the preliminary stages is mighty important; the pressures of the schedule disperse the various departments to their separate chores, perhaps not to reconvene until technical rehearsals. This skimpiness of communication among the staff due to work pressures explains a phenomenon that galls the young striving to break into our strange business: the same old combinations of producer-director-designer repeat show after show, season after season. It may well be a retrogressive formula, but there is safety in a team that knows what everyone else is doing off in their rehearsal halls and shops—they know because they have been there before. In the commercial theatre security is precious.

The color rendering of the set may or may not precede the early conferences. There is nothing like a pretty picture to ensure approval and the go-ahead, so time permitting, a flossy, matted, cellophaned sketch will facilitate matters.

There are lots of rendering techniques, but there is a reason for the persistent popularity of the translucent water color. Its luminosity and airiness captures the quality of the finished setting under stage lights. No opaque medium approximates the shimmering illusion of incandescent bulbs. Water color is a difficult and elusive instrument to master, but there is no decent substitute. The designer need not concern himself with scientific color theory beyond simple knowledge of the color wheel with its primaries and complementaries. You will be handling highly impure pigments, and confusion is compounded beyond repair by the mixture of equally impure colored light media and the unanalyzable welter of materials, fabrics, makeup, etc. Once there was a craze for elaborate model stages with little light units and switchboards and everything. Quite fascinating, but the rationale of being able to scale down color just

101, 102

Howard Bay   "Carmen"   [sumi painting]   (San Francisco, 1961)

doesn't hold up. The variables are beyond calculation. For one thing, a tiny light bulb does not emit the same color as a 1000-watt spot and, then, how does one dilute color media so that a miniature will duplicate the full-size thing—not to mention the color distortions from lenses, reflectors and dust in the atmosphere. I am afraid that only the sloppy, trial-and-error method piles up a working familiarity with the behavior of color onstage. Another pointless tangent is the symbolism of color, because there are no universal color associations. So the impressive color systems remain in the library, and we pass on to art materials.

Water colors are available in cakes, tubes and bottles. Cake pans are messy and unsatisfactory. Winsor and Newton tubes are of good quality and come in many colors. They may be supplemented by the intense inks in bottles put out by Dr. Martin. A range of shades is necessary because mixtures may end up lifeless and dull, and some of the brightest aniline inks do not mix at all. A tube of absolutely opaque white rounds out the palette. Brushes are important and must be handled with love. Winsor and Newton sables in about half a dozen sizes will do nicely. Paper is a question of preference. I use a rough surface, but many favor illustration boards. Anyway, it is simpler and speedier, if more expensive, to buy backed paper unless one is taken with the mystique of wetting, stretching and taping water-color paper. If so, consult a manual on water-color painting, such as *The Technique of Water Colour Painting* by Richmond and Littlejohns.

Any session with water colors should start off with warming-up exercises of brushwork on scraps of water-color board, lest you ruin the sketch. The sketch itself, which is drawn in outline to one-half-inch scale on tracing paper, is transferred to the board with graphite paper. Graphite paper permits some erasures; the oils in carbon paper repel color. A ballpoint pen makes transfer easy; what has been traced can be easily distinguished from the untouched pencil outline. Drawing directly on the board is not a good idea, because erasures chew up the delicate surface of water-color paper.

It is the nature of water color to have a tossed-off, spontaneous appearance; anything laborious or patched up betrays the medium. This air of careless ease is hard to come by and often several discarded sketches strew the floor. The added constriction of having all details in exact scale doesn't help attain a breezy flourish. What does help is laying in the broad areas of a background first and gradually working forward to the downstage minutiae. Only practice will tell you how wet the initial wash should be, although usually before painting you will want to dampen the board completely with clean water evenly distributed with your largest brush. More drawing can be done anytime along the way with a pen dipped into Dr. Martin inks. These lines can be bled with water.

Howard Bay "Music Man" [sumi painting] (New York, 1957)

Howard Bay "Casey Jones" [show curtain: pastel, dyes and opaques]

Carl Kent "Cyrano" [opaques] (1946)

Howard Bay *"Show Boat"* *[opaques]* *(New York, 1946)*

There is a contradiction in a tinted sketch on white paper promising the final appearance of a scene on the stage picked out from darkness by light. Every so often someone gleefully tries to break this impasse by working up the design with opaque paint on a black ground. The result is not only a funereal, depressing article but the expanse of black is a positive weight, while onstage the absence of light is a negative, peripheral phenomenon unnoticed in the spectator's concentration on the illuminated areas. The problem is simply taken care of by the long-accepted convention that scenic designs are water-color sketches on white paper, period. Don't laugh, for you will discover that deviations from the traditional fuzzy painting, from Inigo Jones through Robert Edmond Jones, through Oenslager and Mielziner, are looked upon as not proper scenic sketches. There is an impending breakup of this attitude, but we will postpone that until the newer stagecraft. For now we shall list certain tricks that aid the sketch in its intention of portraying the ultimate setting. The hard edge and every little detail and dark corner precisely completed will destroy the proportion between important and unimportant components. Foreground figures, objects and furniture should have a halo around them, some air and space to set them off. Cheesecloth and blotters can pick up the wet wash, leaving the foreground clean. Only significant matter

Howard Bay   "Night of the Auk"   [sketch]   (New York, 1956)

Howard Bay   "Night of the Auk"   [model]   (New York, 1956)

should be incisively starred, with sharp tonal contrasts limited to the significant shapes. In order to reserve strong accents for key items, the background and middle distance should be handled in a limited range of color and value and with a falling off in definition. Your color palette should be settled prior to touching the sketch with a brush. The strip of color swatches is at your elbow as you daub away. The use of a monochromatic line throughout pulls things together. If you study color sketches by leading designers you will note the very limited palettes used, most judiciously touched up with chalky white highlights, but splurges of vibrant, rich color are rare. A riot of color is seldom an aid to dramaturgy.

The simple rule of the projection of the warm end of the spectrum and the recession of the cool end, plus a familiarity with value, hue and saturation, are all the book learning you need to supplement constant practice with water colors. Hue is simply a color's position on the spectrum. Value is its blackness or whiteness, and saturation is its intensity.

A perusal of examples of water-color techniques through the centuries wouldn't be amiss. Start with   104
eighteenth century Venetians, the nineteenth century English (Turner, Nash, et al.) and such near   105
contemporaries as the late Hood and her imitators in those Lord and Taylor ads, plus George Grosz, Topolski, Rex Whistler, John Piper. We are talking about water colors, but personally I have found one sure cure for a tight, finicky rendering bind: periodic immersion in Eastern brushwork. The discipline of sumi   106
ink, rice paper and the enforced, irrevocable spontaneity of the method loosen up the cramped hand and the cautious mind. There are too few teachers of merit. The best substitute is Tuttle's publication, *Japanese Ink-Painting* by Ryukyu Saito. If you become hooked on the sensuous feeling of that velvety ink on that sensitive paper you might like to read *The Way of the Brush* by Van Briessen. Actually, sketches are   108
possible on rice paper; I put the San Francisco Opera Company's set and costume designs for *Carmen* and   109
the costume plates for *The Man of La Mancha* on rice paper.

As a departure from pure water-color rendition, I have found it worthwhile under the pressure of knocking out colored sketches to combine pastels and water colors. This method demands a rough surface   110
paper that will hold the pastel. After the drawing is transferred to the board, pastels are applied for the airbrush-type blending and under-painting. Stumps grind the pastel into the paper, so there is no dust hanging on the surface, erasers wipe out the superfluous, a brush flicks any loose powder off, a very light fixative is sprayed on, and the entire procedure of water-color painting begins with this subtle, fused base of pastel shading underneath. An interplay of color is possible by using contrasting colors in the pastel undercoat and the water-color overcoat. A relatively hard pastel, such as Nupastel, tends to stay put on the paper. The eraser is an important tool in blending and picking out highlights. This pastel-water-color combination will not work if the pastel isn't embedded in the paper. Too great dependence on pastel and a slighting of water color is the line of least resistance, but the completed design will be weak and characterless. Only the brush can make a dashing statement.

Naturally, scripts come along that make the posteresque quality of opaque colors mandatory. Many of the   111
acrylic products (Bocur Aquatec, Numaster, Permanent Pigments) offer a tremendous flexibility and range of effects. Guides to handling acrylics are found in handbooks such as *Painting with Acrylics* by Guterrez and Roukes. Transparent and opaque may be used in a single sketch. Perhaps transparent for soft distances and for elusive light rays, while blocks of strong definition sans atmosphere are put down with opaques. Finely ground good opaques are worth the extra cost; many cheap poster colors are merely dyes padded

out with fillers and binders, and attempts to mix them lead to unpleasant surprises. If you go in for fancy relief with gesso or Sobo you will need to purchase a bottle of No Crawl fluid to mix with your pigments (unless you use acrylics that have their own plastic medium). Also No Crawl will anchor color to most water-repellent surfaces, such as plastics. Always remember that a color-rendering is made for no other purpose than to project the appearance of the final setting complete with furnishings and light. If it also serves as an indication of the execution, that is peachy, but more often than not detailed color elevations must be painted up to guide the scenic artists. Pointers on such scenic elevations later.

112   Finished color models are coming back in vogue as substitutes for color sketches. We have gone full circle; in the early decades of the century and into the '20s, before the freelance designers, models were the thing. The model-making room of the scenic studio pasted up models based on the director's ground plan and the studio's own research. The pretty miniature was carted off to the producer for approval, then returned to the shop where the working drawings were made, and eventually the flats were painted from the model. The return of the model has a logic. The raw, unpainted cardboard affair has always been around for figuring out a complex structure or aiding the director in plotting his traffic. The shriveling of purely pictorial background scenics and the mushrooming of open stages with their plastic elements and use of found objects have done the trick. Plus the fact that the commercial shops have taken over most of the drafting and now accept the model from the designer and continue the work from that point on. A sizable percentage of these models are more sculpture than a succession of planes in the peephole tradition. Plaster, carved balsa wood, celastic, wire, styrofoam and just strange scraps make up the components stuck to the stage platform. Most of the techniques involved come under prop-making, but a word of caution; those intriguing found materials that look spiffy in the model better be reproducible in full size on the stage. I would hate to see you striving to manufacture a ten-foot-high brooch set with a moss agate. Models are always real cute but they are time-consuming and expensive; allow space on the production calendar. Also, believe it or not, models in their solid way are just as deceptive as sketches.

Theatrical drafting divides into two categories: (1) the designer's plans and elevations and (2) the shop working drawings. Both are simple compared to architectural or engineering drafting and call for a minimum of structural and mathematical calculations. The designer's drawings diagram precisely what the designer wants and no more. They cover the profile and outside dimensions of all elements and show where and how they function in the running order. They are a complete portrayal of all the finished items in the physical production, but they do not specify how anything is to be constructed or the breakdown into manageable units. The designer's tracings portray what is visible on the front—the audience—side of the scenery. The shop layout man takes over the designer's prints and converts them into building drawings.

Drafting equipment is elementary: a drawing board or table (preferably a table) at least 31 inches by 42 inches to accommodate half-inch plans of most backstages; a T-square to match; an adjustable triangle with a built-in protractor; a scale ruler; a pink eraser; a pencil compass and a bow compass; a drafting lamp; a 30-inch roll of thin, tough, transparent tracing paper (not vellum, which smudges); drafting pencils and sandpaper blocks for pointing same. Mechanical drafting pencils are the approved instruments, but I plod along with two Scripto mechanical pencils—one soft for sketching and heavy lines and one harder for everything else. Being thin leads they do not require sharpening. Of course there are impressive gadgets, such as electric pencil sharpeners and erasers and all sorts of templates, but who needs them?

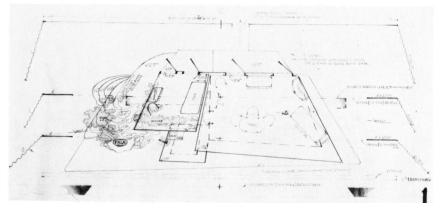

Howard Bay   "A Certain Joy"   [plan]

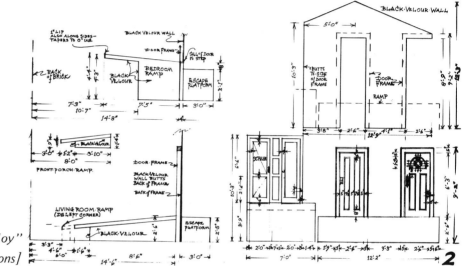

Howard Bay   "A Certain Joy"   [elevations]

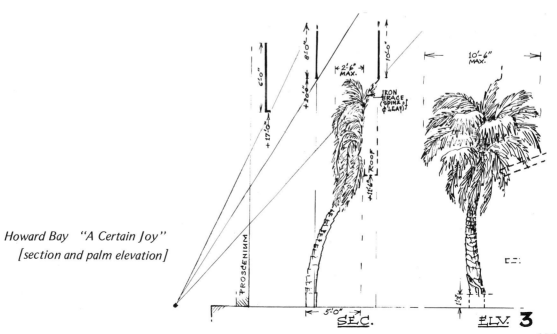

Howard Bay   "A Certain Joy"   [section and palm elevation]

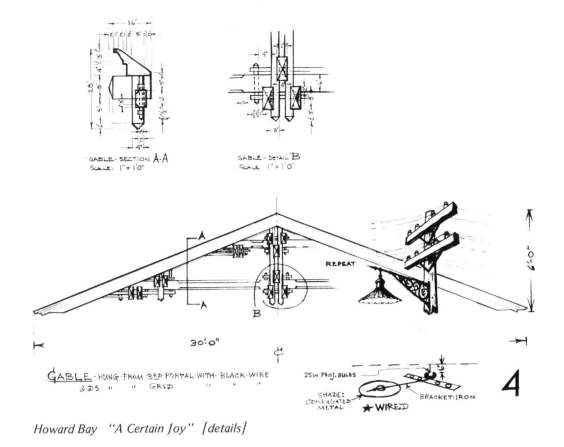

GABLE · SECTION A·A
SCALE: 1"=1'0'

GABLE · DETAIL B
SCALE 1"=1'0'

REPEAT

30'0"

GABLE·HUNG·FROM·3RD·PORTAL·WITH·BLACK·WIRE
& DS " " GRID " "

25W PROJ. BULBS

SHADE:
CORRUGATED
METAL
★ WIRED

BRACKET: IRON

4

Howard Bay "A Certain Joy" [details]

Howard Bay "A Certain Joy" [finished set]

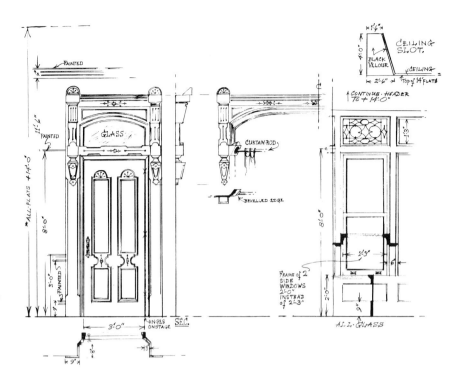

Howard Bay   "Midsummer" [details]

The purpose of a designer's drawings is to furnish the execution departments with simple, crystal-clear, artistic directives, not to exhibit technical expertise; the shop craftsmen probably have forgotten more about mechanical matters than you will ever know. One does consult the shop specialists in the process of designing and drafting, asking questions about this or that piece of machinery or an untried use of some material. The boundaries of what is possible are stretched through this interchange. Never forget for a fleeting moment that these shop characters who could be linesmen for the Jets, are very stage-struck gents who enjoy unraveling a knotty technical puzzle.

First, the rough ground plan that received the director's approval is made fresh and neat and exact in half-inch scale with a corresponding sectional view to check heights, masking and room for lights. The section is rapidly drawn on a tracing over the plan with the floor line coinciding with the center line on the plan. Horizontal sight lines are determined on the plan from the side seats in the first row of the orchestra. Vertical sight lines noted on the section are taken from the first row in the orchestra and from the back row in the balcony. A low-hung balcony may obstruct sight for those at the back of the orchestra floor. The portal height, or whatever establishes the front trim, is a balance between sight lines and the ideal opening for the show. Heights are deceptive. A sixteen-foot-high opening seems much higher when hung in the air than when you view the portal lying on the shop floor. A couple of feet must be added to the height of masking to allow for actual sight lines, which are on the diagonal and not what you have drawn at center on a plane perpendicular to the curtain line. Be rather lavish with masking generally; it has a tendency to get hung differently than predicted. Borders and legs get pushed around out of the halation and spill from light pipes and booms. Masking is usually dead black or deep blue velour (lined for opacity). Once there were neutral gray drapes but that is impossible; gray drapes were visibly there and thereby could not be neutral. Only an absence of light achieves neutrality. By the way, borders are horizontal pieces of cloth that are

117

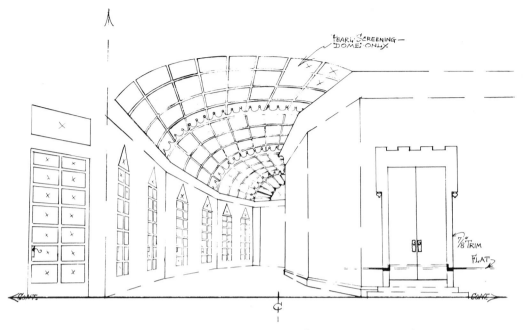

Lemuel Ayres   "Bloomer Girl"   [framed drop elevation]   (New York, 1944)

Prop drawing

Howard Bay   "Carmen Jones"   [house unit]   (New York, 1945)

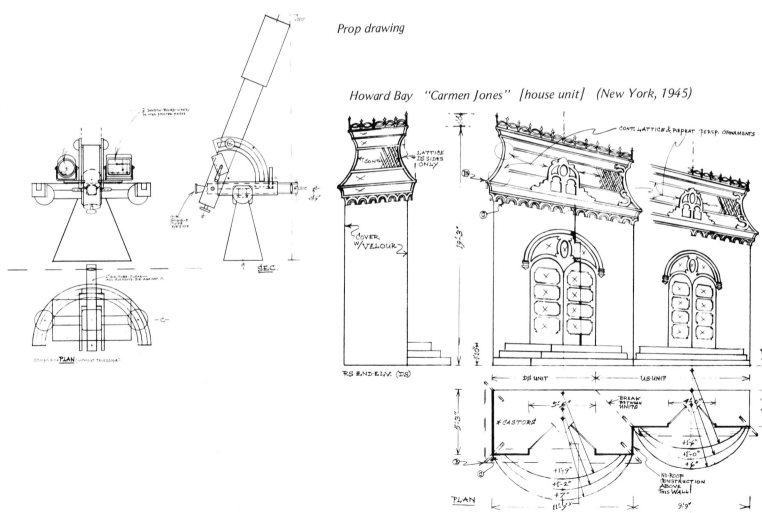

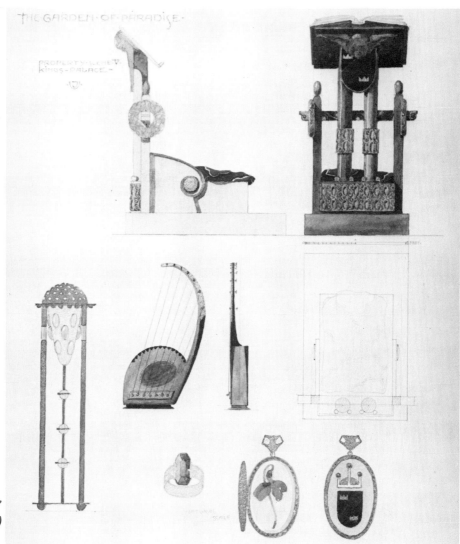

Joseph Urban "Garden of Paradise"
[props] (1914)

hung up high and block out the gridiron and mask light pipes and any hanging scenery. Legs are vertical strips hung to the floor up and downstage on the sides to blot out the offstage and any boomerang and ladder lights.

Before carefully lettering in all your notes and ruling borders around the plan and section you should move on to the elevations, because they are apt to alter the plan and section. The elevations are nothing more than flattened-out pieces of the set, also drawn in half-inch scale, running around the stage from downright to downleft. You start at the top left corner of a clean sheet of tracing paper and keep going. If the show is a standard interior (which it seldom is these days) the set itself may fit into two rows on one sheet; the portal, maskings, backings and soft goods on another; and any specially built props on other sheets. Details, depending on their intricacy, may be blown up to one and a half or three inches to the foot or full scale. Usually the full scale is left to the scenic artists, subject to a check by the designer. Only half of a portal need be drawn if it is symmetrical; soft masking and drops, if there are no irregularities in profiles; no cuts or appliques, may be listed with dimensions, which avoids having to draw many large blank rectangles. All dimensions are carried outside the scenic pieces. Notes are frugal and used only in referring to departures from the norm. Isometric projection is a method for visualizing a three-dimensional unit and even an entire setting, but it is an unnatural device that doesn't conform to the workings of the human eye. If the combination of plan, frontal elevation and side view doesn't clarify a complex object, a freehand sketch is appropriate. Irregular props can be drawn freehand if the basic dimensions are superimposed—and if you frequent the shop during the progress of the building as you are supposed to do.

Drafting is not an automatic, insensitive transfer operation but an extension of the design process. Aesthetic decisions are made with every mark of pencil on paper. If part or all of the drafting is relegated to assistants, the designer must check and refine every square inch or the quality of the original conception will evaporate and you will be saddled with sterile blobs of inert scenery. Elevations not only demand the manipulation of a T-square and triangle but often embody as much freehand skill as the sketch. This is one more reason not to lean too heavily on a crude model that is apt to lose the precision of the controlled contour. Quarter-inch scale models are darling and portable but are much too petit to convey delicacy of detail. Even rough half-inch scale models should be converted into elevations or an absolutely finished, colored model before consignment to the tender mercies of the shops.

Donald Oenslager "Tosca" [scenic color elevation] (1966)

Claude Bragdon "Ruy Blas" [scenic color details] (New York, 1933)

To prepare color elevations for the scenic studio, transfer all half-inch elevations to water-color board. Here one has to be considered and precise—none of the fuzz and atmosphere of the rendering. The spirit of the rendering must be translated into exact guides for the scenic artists—scaled statements in paint. The looseness of washes can be preserved by masking around the outlines of the units and brushing with abandon. On paper, you need not match too literally the media actually used by the artists because they will sense what is best expressed in heavy or thin paint, opaques, dyes, or whatever. Just put down what you wish the scenery to look like.

Once you have dutifully delivered all sketches, working drawings, samples, etc., to the scenic shop you have only completed a healthy portion of your task. The profusion of accessories, the furniture, draperies, upholstery and dressing are crucial. Drama is more dependent on the things the actors handle and sit on

George Jenkins   "Annie Get Your Gun" [scenic color elevations] (Los Angeles 1957)

Page references for illustration

than on the walls back there. Often there are no walls back there like in the Old Days. Primarily you are collecting ready-mades from hither and yon. This can get out of hand without your being aware of it until it's too late to patch it up. Prop chasing has none of the cozy reflection of the studio, where all your scenic pieces are spread out on the drawing board, encompassed by a single glance. The rightness of a chair, and the rightness of that chair with the scores of things yet to be unearthed, is decided by nothing but vague feelings. The only insurance that these feelings won't let you down is a never-ending study of periods and furnishings—in fact, of all the baggage with which people surround themselves. High-class designers are burdened with an avid, unnatural curiosity trained on all the tasteful and distasteful possessions that humankind grasps to its bosom. In scrounging for props you are very much at the mercy of your locale. Antique merchants who condescend to rent to Those Theatre People are well-nigh indispensable. The dragon ladies and pastel courtiers who deal in antiques must be cultivated as artfully as the Leading Figures on the Board of Trustees. That is the provincial situation; in New York City there are the Newel Art Galleries, a fascinating storehouse of oddities from all periods and in-between periods, managed by non-temperamental, efficient people who specialize in theatre, film, TV, display, and photo rentals. They pack properly and are ready for the truck tomorrow morning at nine, rental towards purchase.

Out there where the stock is not so rich and the designer has to make do, emphasize a few key pieces and strive manfully to avoid Salvation Army Victorian where an earlier period is stipulated in the text. A shop-made cube is preferable to the wrong chair; except for working props strike anything that exudes misleading connotations. Somehow one can juggle carpentry and paint and surmount all sorts of limitations of personnel and budget in scenery, but there is a stone wall if one needs a Louis XV settee and there doesn't seem to be one in the vicinity. Actors cannot sit on a projection of a settee, so delegate prop procurement to personable diplomats and dispatch them into the field early in rehearsals. They are only scouts because you must make the final choice. Tender care and the prompt return of borrowed finery keep channels open for the future; handing out comps and gratuities is a shrewd investment, and the business manager must be made to see the logic of this largesse.

124

If you have dutifully scaled your furniture on plan and elevations and have done your work on the prop lists at rehearsal with the director, the stage manager and your prop man, you should knock off the better part of your needs quickly. Check off the items that do not require your aesthetic judgment, and the prop man will track them down. Good prop men are ingenious procurers, crammed full of clues to the whereabouts of the most esoteric of the world's goods. If Joe Lynn didn't return by the stroke of twelve with a left-sided opium bed with pearl inlay, one feared the worst. The approved mixture is a prop man who is a superior shopper and an assistant who is a superlative mechanic. For the specialty shops devoted to prop-making have all gone away, and the scenic shops resent and sidetrack those finicky, time and space-consuming knicknacks—particularly if the designer is an agreeable chap who doesn't nudge the shop into making room. The prop man will arrange all trucking, such as the delivery of things that must be rebuilt to the scenic shop and furniture requiring upholstery to the drapery shop. Having picked out your materials at the fabric houses you dump the cuttings at the drapery shop who calculates the yardage and orders it. Don't feel deprived if the management does not look kindly on $75.00-a-yard Scalamandre silk brocade—there are acceptable substitutes on the market—no paying customer will be within thirty feet of the fine needlework. Draperies must project a strong silhouette. Err on the side of oversized trimmings. The thickness of the material, liberal yardage, lining and interlining, weights and chains give and hold the proper bulk and plasticity. These matters are understood by theatrical drapery firms. Another matter that they alone accept is an unreasonable delivery date, but remember that they are at the mercy of dyers and vendors who saunter along on nontheatrical timetables. An upholstery hint: hard, high seats. Equity members do not like to sink into luxurious downy cushions—they are too damn difficult to climb out of gracefully. Be extra-careful that a high-sheen, loud fabric doesn't end up on an outsized sofa down center. All materials should lie quietly back in close-family range and not flaunt one's taste as a decorator. The choosing of fabrics is the dangerous time when designers most often forget themselves and are carried away by a particularly attractive bolt of cloth. Coordinate all materials with the costume designer; not only for color but for blends and contrasts of textures and for reflective properties. Teamwork between the set designer and the costume designer is crucial. Theoretical arguments for the scenery and the clothes to be drawn up by a single artist cannot be disputed but in practice there is rarely time to do both jobs. If you dig into the facts behind the credit "Settings and Costumes Designed by So-and-so," you will usually find that So-and-So delegated to able assistants most of the work on either the settings or the costumes. Overseeing costume workrooms and covering fitting appointments is a full-time worry; in the scenic shop one isn't called upon to woo actresses who just never wear green. Either designer may develop the color scheme initially. The designers cross-check not only the sketches but all samples and swatches. Store bought clothes are harder to coordinate than shop constructed costumes but colors mustn't get out of control. It is indeed fortunate when a compatible pair of set and costume designers can labor together for many seasons. A panel's worth of any expanse of drapery should be tried under the color media in the electrical shop.

Pictures are scene-stealers and should be used gingerly if they don't perform in the action; ways and means must be found for minimizing and/or eliminating large framed affairs and segregating clusters of small frames away from center stage. Practical light fixtures must be so distributed as to give motivating excuses for area lighting control. The balance of luminosity through wattage and shade translucency is

Newel Art Galleries (New York)

delicate. All ceramics, glass and glossy bulk must be warily chosen; if sparkle is called for it should be controllable—counting the balcony pan lamps in the glass doors of the secretary or watching a silver pitcher act like the Montauk lighthouse does take away from the words.

Whenever possible the inexperienced designer should arrange the furnishings in their stage relationship during selection; disparate scale and shape can make uncongenial playmates. The transition between neighboring pieces is even more critical on an open stage than in the enclosed box. Don't wind up with wooden soldiers just standing there. Soft filigreed outlines, and greenery if appropriate, slur edges with nonchalant overlaps; opaque lumps expose the skeleton set. Some pieces can be naturally skeletonized by removing panels and backings. The open set demands a tight unity of style; closure with walls is in itself an adhesive. By the way, receive permission to paint rented articles; it would be a shame to spend the best years of your life paying off the evaluation on a defiled credenza.

High on the list of irritating services are the purveyors of artificial foliage to the theatre. They subscribe to the limited view that nature is stamped out of old window shades. You may have bigger or smaller leaves but they all are haphazardly wired onto spindly branches that in turn are stuck on lumpy papier-mache stumps. The way to avoid these artisans is (1) make friends in the flower market and purchase good materials directly; (2) insist that the scenic shop assign a sculptor for modeling trees.

You will find yourself doing a lot of insisting in the shops. There are easier and faster methods of doing almost anything, but compromises in the product cannot be explained away in program notes—it is your name up there amongst the hairdressers' and production assistants'. Even in dealing with bosom companions it is smart to have evidence in writing—memos on changes, alterations on dated prints—not left to chancy phone calls and unconfirmed conversations. The icky sentimentality of Tony Award gambols does not operate in the workaday theatre.

Interspersed with the hectic shopping and shop visiting, you should pay daily calls on rehearsals; changes do arise that need instant attention or the backlash is ferocious. Altogether this depressing period of loose ends and scattered worrisome fragments, and will it all get finished and dumped on the trucks, plagues the artistic temperament to the bursting point. Steel yourself, wheedle, cajole and finally demand that it be right and complete, and you are on the way to becoming a designer. We assume you have the requisite talent, but the concrete product must arrive onstage and all elements appear to belong together in this one theatrical venture.

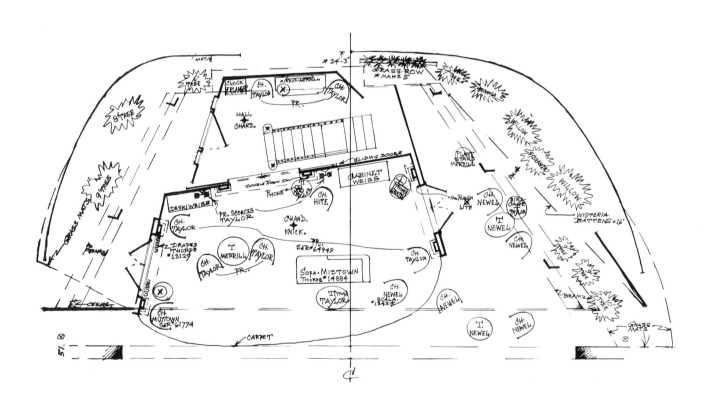

Howard Bay "Autumr Garden" [props and upholstery] (New York, 1951)

IV.
The Execution of One's Handiwork

How much should a designer concern himself with the detailed workings of the shops? Are the professional service studios the shining ideal? Does one mechanically shrink the scale for noncommercial ventures? What hallowed shop procedures are likely to disappear tomorrow? What industrial and engineering marvels may be lifted for theatrical use, or is the basically handicraft thinking of the stage right and proper for all time? Or is the primitive mode of making things dictated by the small change to be had for dramatic furnishings? These are the questions for the designer—not when to use a number nine wood screw.

The designer need not know how to hold a hammer or how to address a band saw and keep ten fingers on his hands. But he should acquire sufficient familiarity with all facets of execution to judge what is possible with existing personnel, equipment, space, time, and budget. Beyond what is given, the resources within the shops, is the whole arena of modern technology. The pendulum has swung back to the medieval guilds after a spell of workshops under royal patronage. In boom times the independent shops were split into specialty outfits: carpentry, painting, props, drapery and upholstery, flower and foliage firms, and outside blacksmiths for metalwork. Then carpenters and painters got together; the prop houses fell apart; the exclusively theatrical foliage-makers evaporated; the carpenters took over the sewing of drops, masking and ground cloths; hauling charges climbed sky-high; show money vanished; and today, the three decent shops in Greater New York just hang on. Out of necessity they have absorbed the various subdivisions of physical production, are shackled by outlandish rents for the vast square footage needed, lay out princely wages and year-round guarantees to hold the skilled help who could drift over to a TV studio and doze on overtime, must borrow considerable sums for new machinery, are on the lookout for vendors in the efficient business world who just might promise delivery a fortnight after St. Swithens, must tie up the trucks awaiting a certified check, are always Taking Care of the police, fire and sundry Public Servants, etc., etc.

The geography of a commercial shop reflects the feast-or-famine theatrical syndrome. Space, machinery and help must be geared to all contingencies, and that can be a heller when five shows descend at once. What is worse, all five may be heavy in the same department, say metalwork. All five may require all-over decks. A rapid calculation multiplying by five the backstage square footage of an average house will give you the open floor space needed to spread out all those decks simultaneously. And if any of the decks incorporate tricky electronic or winch mechanisms, guess how many working days said decks will be spread around? Add to that the need for generous open space all on one floor with at least twenty-foot heights, lots of power with outlets everywhere and large loading doors; the traffic pattern from drawing board through wood-working, covering, metal-working, prop-building, the paint shop, the drapery and upholstery section to the load-out door. It is absolutely essential to have all benches, templates, palettes and machinery on casters and all materials off the floor in compact but handy racks, thus permitting the shift of priorities to the busy departments. The only stationary islands may be the office-drafting room, where the designer's

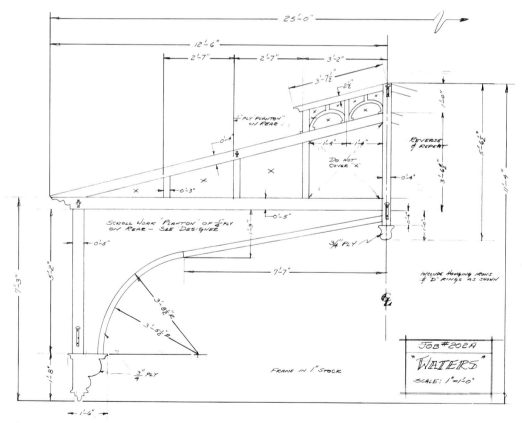

Doug Maddox   Shop drawing

stuff is converted into shop drawings and the work is farmed out; the tool-hardware storage; and the locker-washrooms.

Let us take a show from the top. The designer spreads out his drawings and models for analysis and estimate. On hand should be the shop head (presumably a master carpenter, a crackerjack mechanic and a grand organizer), the chargeman scenic artist and the soft-goods man. This group should be augmented by specialists if there are strange problems beyond the expertise of the first team. The analysis-estimate ritual cannot be relegated to amateurs, salesmen or front men. The chore must be assumed by the brains who are not only knowledgeable but are responsible for the product. This point can be checked by recourse to the records of bankrupt scenic firms.

The designer not only unfurls his art but explains which theatres have been booked; delivery dates; set-up time; the running order; the maximum number of bodies atop weight-bearing units; the expected time for each scene change and whether they are open changes; the management's calculation of crew size; the placement of switchboards in each move; whether there will be extra impedimenta backstage, such as animals, dressing rooms, musicians; and generally how everything works and what needs to be practical or terribly solid or light as a feather.

The shop side asks questions, because no blueprint has been devised that anticipates all contingencies. In fact, as noted in the design process chapter, the designer's drawings display only what the finished settings should look like and how they function, plus mention of any special materials desired.

The meeting is adjourned; the shop pieces together an estimate composed in the usual manner of estimating man hours, materials, overhead and profit. Unlike the subjects of other estimates, no show is identical with any other show. P.S. There are no rich scenic contractors. The estimate is presented to the management; they shout that they could build a house for that sum. The shop counters with, "Not delivered in New Haven in three weeks you couldn't." And the whittling away at the extravagant designer starts. There are ways to cut back on costs, some logical and some illogical. In the commercial framework it is foolhardy to eliminate any mechanics that will ultimately pile on more expensive manpower in the theatre; a thousand-dollar saving in manufacture is eaten up in a few weeks of performances. The initial cost is not as vital as the operational cost—a maxim difficult to impress on neophyte producers of plays. Also time should not be wasted fuming about the justice of the union's arbitrary decrees on how many stagehands are required backstage. The only constructive counterattack is to kill the need for any help in a specific location: in the flys, upstage, right stage or left stage. The shop can come through with sensible shortcuts: doubling units with minor design modifications, trading in large framed units for soft hangings that are not only easier to produce but do not take time and stage floor space to assemble. Is your heart set on a cumbersome facade even though an entranceway is all that actually performs in the action? In the conceptual period authors, producers, directors and ofttimes designers are more literal minded than the ultimate audience. The author fixed a complete, specific locale in his mind's eye, but the spectator's attention seldom strays far beyond the atmosphere engendered by the items the actors cope with. Focus is dissipated by towering bulk lumbering on and off stage. Wouldn't a nice leaf pattern projected over that porch cancel out all the dead foliage? Isn't that elaborately modeled ground row rather corny—and distracting to boot? Will the audience appreciate your incorporation of genuine mahogany veneer thirty feet upstage of the curtain line? It all calms down; contracts are signed; there is even less time to knock out the production, and in the meantime the shop has taken on a thirty-six-scene venture for the Alex Cohen office.

Our sole concern is with the designer as supervisor of execution. If company B is awarded the contract and is weak in some area you must insist that the firm hire the right craftsmen, or that they subcontract that section of the job to someone who is competent in the specialty required. Life is more pleasant if you have made this stipulation clear at estimating time.

127

Before the layout drawings (which break down the scenery into manageable segments and specify all construction details) are distributed you must check to avoid obvious cracks. You discuss butt joints or lap joints, the spacing of visible cables and how to disguise visible braces. Certain members may need beefing up for support or rigidity—the shop knows best, so do a little redrafting. After the scenic artists have drawn up the full-size patterns, you check them before they reach the carpenters. This is an important task, because the precise contour is not very plain in half-inch scale. The standard flatwork and the platform bulk need not take up your valuable time, but you should hover over the trim, both wood and metal, and all sculptured pieces. Metalwork, which plays a leading role these days both structurally and as skeletal tracery, must be watched; bent tubing can appear particularly graceless if it isn't the right gauge or if a full-size pattern has not been provided. If you have left the choice of special hardware until now, you may settle for second best; but if you keep an up-to-date file of molding, hardware, and decorative trim catalogs the right numbers would be included in your drawings.

Not only direct sculpting hacked out of styrofoam but vacuum-form casting and the pouring and spraying of polyurethane foam has become the rage. Intricate, lightweight repeats in casting and the building up of 3-D shapes by spraying have supplanted the laborious framing, chicken wire and gooked lumps of yesteryear. Just be certain that the modeling in styrofoam or polyurethane is bold enough to shine through the cloth skin that is needed to seal the surface against rough handling in trouping.

There is a special intimacy between the designer and the scenic artist; they are fellow artists meeting on common ground. Scenic painting is a sensitive and highly skilled craft with a very long history. Our studios are a blend of La Scala trained Italians, Austrians and Germans imported by Urban, and landscape painters from London, particularly those from the D'Oyly Carte. To these schools must be added a few Franco-Russians who studied under Schervakbidge, the great executor of the Ballet Russe sets, and the native itinerant journeymen who wandered from stock house to stock house.

In the bustle of manufacturing working drawings and covering all work in progress the designer tends to lean too heavily on the scenic artist's expertise by sloughing off paint elevations and other matter he dumps on the paint shop. Artists have covered up for designers on occasion but it's a chancy thing. The artist may gallop off with many tasteful improvements if the sketch material isn't unified and frightfully clear. Raw research should not be handed over unless you desire an exact copy of such research. Retribution will be swift if a designer airily waves his hand accompanied with the line, "Oh, paint it sort of between Bonnard and maybe Turner, yes, Turner, but for the drawing follow this photo."

Though we are concerned with designer-shop interplay, it should be bluntly stated that no manual can provide instructions for the painting of stage scenery. There is no known substitute for a protracted apprenticeship to a master scenic artist. For a simple glossary of available paints and equipment see *Scenic Artists' Handbook* put out by Gothic Color Co.

A lot of the floor space in our barn-like studios is devoted to painting of drops, which are tacked onto the deck. Floor painting allows freedom of brushwork. Only the Metropolitan Opera House (in New York) still uses paint frames that are a hangover from the tight, dry, detail-by-detail, piecemeal rendition of old-fashioned scenery. Because the separate steps along the way, such as priming, drawing, mixing color, laying in and finishing, are carried out by different artists the designer channels his directives and criticism through the chargeman scenic artist, who carries the burden of both the artistic quality and the cost control of the job. The wide-open, multiple choice, interpretive nature of scenic painting springs from the tremendous disparity between the half-inch-scale sketch and the full-size product; key decisions coloring the intent and spirit of the design rest with the many painters laboring on the actual setting. The choice of paints or dyes; whether to use brushes, sprays or sponge mops and pounces or stencils; the very priming and preparation of the ground are aesthetic points reflecting the rapport between designer and studio. The designer should be up on the virtues of the caseins, latexes and vinyls that are replacing dry pigments and glue size. Vinyl, for instance, is a water-based paint, either flat or gloss, that makes a tough surface for platforms; the clear variety is a binder for bronzing powders and, mixed with anilines, gives a brilliant, clear finish to Plexiglas and other plastics.

It is wise to hang around for the trial assembly in the shop; your maiden view of the composition of the concrete set may hold surprises in scale and in the juxtaposition of elements that were not revealed in the blueprints. This is the moment for renovations, with expert help and machinery at hand, rather than struggle with local artisans and hand tools in the theatre. You should run interference for your property master in his valiant fight to force the shop to pay attention to his worrisome widgets. Oversee the sewing of curtains with particular regard to fullness, draping, lining and weights, so that the valence doesn't end up looking like a giant's bib that an elephant sat on. Make certain that your precious handiwork is snugly fitted with crates, coverings and traveling strips for its journeys.

These hints (and many more) are all well and good, but what does one do about a Glaring Deficiency in the best of professional shops? Scenic firms have grown from the venerable flats-and-drops carpentry shops. They have adapted by necessity and reluctantly to contemporary design demands, grumbling all the while about new-fangled plastics and crazy bent-wire Meccano sets that they would lug home to the kids if the damn things would fit into the basement. The carpenters, who still run things and who have done an amazing job solving the most convoluted technical puzzles involving lumber and rigging, can't face the incontestable fact that they are just not up to dealing with the electronic gear demanded by today's theatrics. The shop presented with the necessity of moving some object by remote control dispatches an apprentice to pick up a secondhand motor that wouldn't have propelled Huck Finn's raft. A percentage of the trouble is the stubborn pride of old craftsmen but a larger percentage can be laid to the pitiful economics that prohibit expenditures for even minimum engineering research. When carpenters and electricians stop pretending they are engineers, there will still remain the question of whether the shops can afford modern electronic engineers. Anyway, until they can, nothing new and dazzling will come to pass in the stage machinery line, and it behooves the designer to be mighty cautious in calling for anything to move differently than it moved in some previous production. It is not difficult to envisage a future rich with simple computers, fluid drive, air cells, etc., which from the scientific view is rather elementary hardware that could dovetail into the handicraft horizons of the scenic business.

No piling up of words and pictures can create a model for planning and operating a shop. The only intelligent guide is a close examination of functioning establishments that grind out a variety of produce. Then one can decide which costly power tools to pass up for the initial installation, particularly if a

Our Author pretends to add the Finishing Touches
(at Nolan Studios)

neighborhood lumber yard will turn out custom work or if there is a smithy for metal fabrication. Drapery and upholstery may be entrusted to decorating trade contractors, but theatrical overseeing is needed.

Non-Broadway varies too widely to set down any rules. Obviously, where the shop adjoins the one and only theatre used, units need not be chopped up into standard portable pieces, and lighter and cheaper materials can replace the rugged materials that traveling scenery demands. A footnote: Schools exist to prepare students for the world outside the schools, so actual samples of the pro way of doing things should be interlarded with cutting up corrugated paper with a sharp knife.

A designer's behavior in the shops has more than a little to do with the quality of the finished article. He should have a genuine regard for fine workmanship, and say so, and strongly insist on patching up shoddy work. Also, flexibility and compromise are not synonymous; changes must be made when time and money are short or when raw material is unavailable, but the audience should not be presented with a smudged carbon of the design concept. Frankly, a designer can do very little when he is saddled with an inferior shop. Furthermore, it is immaterial whether the shop can't do a first-rate job or just doesn't care. There are definite limits to supervision because other bodies are doing the concrete labor. The best shops have failings to which the designer must adjust, by-passing the weak arm and throwing the weight of execution into the strong departments. (I wonder if that is why we see so little scenic painting outside the larger centers of theatrical activity.)

To recap: Beyond a more contemporary outlook on finding better power instruments, the current drift is away from wood turning to sculpting and casting, to metals including patented scaffolding, and to the general airiness that plastics and thin skeletons can offer. The designer would be advised to keep up with the latest architectural products.

V.
Lighting Design

The limitless possibilities of modern lighting have created a mystique of Light as Saviour— the successor to dead architecture, paint and all mundane, literal solids. The recurring phrase: A Lonely Figure Isolated in a Limitless void by a Single Shaft of Searing Light sums it up. Correction: It summarized the Romantic Tradition prior to the Multi-Media Era. Heady stuff, very thrilling, but not too helpful when one is called upon to provide the lighting for a show on a stage. The other side of the coin is equally dangerous: the gadgetry fetish, that good old American pastime, the fascination with electronic toys. The unexciting fact is that light is a worthy handmaiden, not The Answer. Light is nothing until it hits something. Therefore: (1) a simple analysis of the purpose of lighting, (2) a listing of the tools, (3) a description of the work process.

The prime function of lighting is to provide visibility—to illuminate actors and their surroundings—and don't forget it. Good illumination achieves a plasticity, a modeling of animate and inanimate objects. The dynamic potential of lighting is realized when the rhythmic changes of light underscore and propel the development of the drama. Any further generalities would be airy fancies, so forward to ways and means.

Most texts go on at length about the physics of light, which is about as profitable as going out into an electrical storm with a kite and a key on the end of a piece of string. Let us acknowledge we are in the second half of the Twentieth Century and the juice is being provided by the power company. If something goes awry you'll have to contact a licensed electrician anyway. If you have a thirst for electrons, ohms and such, see Theodore Fuch's *Stage Lighting*. The best lighting text is Pilbrow's *Stage Lighting. The Magic of Light,* by Jean Rosenthal and Lael Wertenbaker, is a memorial to Jean the lovely, incandescent person. The meat is scanty: a few solid light plots, focusing schedules and board hook-ups.

We cannot plunge into the design of lighting without familiarity with the tools that create light. We will split coverage of the plumbing into two blocks, dealing first with the instruments that are the primary tools of the designer and holding control systems until after the plot has been turned over to the electrician.

Incandescent housings divide into spotlights, floodlights and special effect and projection units.

First off, we should dispose of general illumination hoods; their use becomes more limited daily. The floodlight, or scoop, is an open Alzac reflector unit of up to 2000 watts that throws an even distribution of light over a large area. Several 300-watt or 500-watt floods arranged in a row within a single housing is called a borderlight, which is usually wired in three circuits. Scoops and borderlights are primarily restricted to cycs (top and bottom and for translucencies) and for an overall smooth coverage of drops. Today the PAR lamps are replacing the bulb plus reflector because the PAR bulb of heavy Pyrex glass has its own built-in reflector. They are available from 75 watts to 1500 watts with 150 watts, 300 watts and 500 watts in common use. They come in both fixed focus flood and fixed focus spot type. They are much more compact than the old troughs. The heat they generate necessitates glass color media. The 500-watt spot strips can be used for backlighting if the throw is not too great. Often two rows are used on a drop; the spot layer tilts down and covers the bottom of the drop and the flood row picks up the top.

The prime hardware consists of beam projectors, Fresnel spots and ellipsoidal spots. A beam projector is a housing of lamp and reflector and no lens. In focus the parabolic reflector sends out parallel rays and the absence of a lens creates a "live" light that is the nearest approximation of sunlight and moonlight. It is bulky, however, and the fixed field of the beam limits its flexibility.

The general utility item is the Fresnel. It is a compact, inexpensive unit that may be spotted or flooded with a beam giving a hot spot and a tapering off at the edges. There is considerable spill, which rules it out for front of the house or where sharp framing is called for. Painting the lens risers with black enamel cuts down on the spill. Its main purpose is easy blending of acting areas; also, it is fine for the soft highlighting of scenery.

Modern stage lighting is dependent on the ellipsoidal spotlight. It is a simple projection system, very efficient, that has a minimum of spill and provides freedom to shape the beam. Of secondary importance, simple slides and masks may be inserted into the aperture gate for rudimentary pattern masking. The proper lenses for different throws are listed in the instrument catalogs. The 1500-watt and 2000-watt ellipsoidals, called cannons, have taken over for backlighting and the long throws of the big open sets. The ellipsoidal is the only instrument for front-of-the-house hanging or in any position where framing and little spill is important.

The returns aren't in yet on the value of the quartz-iodine bulbs, and the zenon bulb (a powerful, concentrated source that is not dimmable) is still too delicate and dangerous for general stage use, although it has proved valuable for projections and in follow spots.

Having lined up our arsenal of lamps we are almost ready to consider the art of lighting a show. The proscenium theatre is still the norm. The commercial playhouse offers the incoming attractions precious little in the electrical line. The antiquated house board handles nothing beyond the house lights and the pitiful glow throughout the dank hallways that the fire department can't very well waive for the standard gratuities. The house electrician who remembers Mr. Belasco, and a perfect gentleman he was too, is always changing the bulbs in the marquee or communing with the ponies. Everything, switchboards, cables, balcony pans, booms, lamps, are lugged up the alley into the stage door, plugged into the main and hauled out again at the end of the run—mighty quaint and backbreaking and expensive and inefficient. Theatre managements detest incoming shows because live shows disturb the quiet, orderly existence of a tenantless house, our Thirty Years' War to take over the boxes for lights so that built-out aprons can be properly lit is a raunchy saga worthy of Tammany Hall.

The above grumbling aside is by way of bringing home the physical limitations confronting the lighting designer before he can put pencil to paper. Equipment in front of the proscenium entails snaking the cable, hanging pans on the face of the balcony so that falling color frames won't dent the noggins of the customers in the expensive seats, erecting box booms (occasionally they are built in, usually in the wrong positions), and hanging, focusing and coloring the lamps themselves. Backstage life is a bit easier; the delicate point is coordination with the carpentry department, which we take up under the setup.

It sounds infantile to spell it out, but it is unavoidable: lighting is hanging the right instrument in the

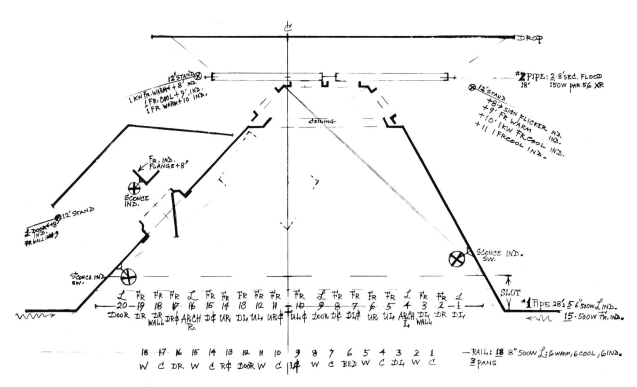

Howard Bay "Midsummer" [box set electrics]

134

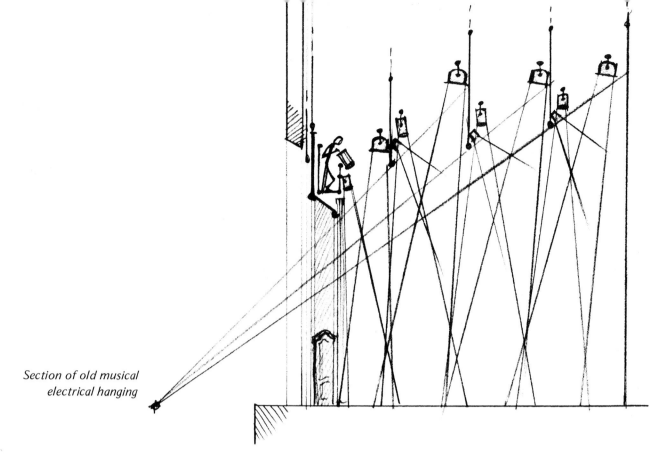

Section of old musical electrical hanging

right place and focusing it at the right target. The reason it must be said is that the haphazard growth of theatrical lighting perpetuates outdated practices, obscuring this simple axiom. The Italianate system of layers of scenery parallel to the footlights had corresponding layers of borderlights for even illumination of the painted acreage. When Naturalism junked the flappy painted cloths, the borderlights were banished upstage to take care of that small patch of sky glimpsed through the curtained window. The box set not only sealed out the backstage but squeezed the light units (the individual spotlight with dimmer control had arrived) into one claustrophobic position, the first pipe embedded in a slot out back into the front of the ceiling. Oh sure, little rays of sunlight and moonlight peeking through apertures in the walls furnished Motivating Sources, and out front a timid wash from the balcony pans wiped out those Unsightly Shadows under the eyes, noses and chins of the Equity members; but the first pipe lit the play. Modeling in a shallow box set was and is limited to the rudimentary stratagem of pairing two lamps spaced right and left on the pipe hitting each section of the stage. Designers and electricians were occupied with lighting plays and didn't disseminate their knowledge, thus leaving the field to a schoolteacher who went and wrote a book on A Method For Lighting the Stage. It is a pity this had to happen. The Method: (A) Divide the stage into a grid of twelve circular Areas, all neatly labeled with large numerals. (B) The spot covering any given Area from one side must be in a warm color and its mate from the other side must be in a cool color. The results: (A) The holes between the Areas must be plugged up with added units, it all ending in an arbitrary patchwork. The static, symmetrical inflexibility of the superimposed Area grid cannot accommodate the varying demands of assorted scripts.(B) Why should an actor be blue when he faces left stage, pink when he faces right stage, and pied when he turns front?

While the pros were laboring on subtle, minor variations inside their scenery boxes and the school children were making circles with their compasses, things were happening in musicals. The layers of scenery parallel to the footlights had been carried over from the hoary opera tradition. The only novelty was a timid updating of the painterly styles on the surfaces. As directors, such as Hassard Short and Murray Anderson, and designers, such as Norman bel Geddes, moved in, the borderlights were retained to light the drops nice and even, but the new spotlights added concentration, atmosphere, and just plain variety. The spots were hung not only in layers in the air next door to the borderlights but also on the boomerangs on the sides behind the wings, thus initiating cross lighting. The opera bridge, masked by an ornate Show Portal, was inhabited by operators who not only manipulated the onstage follow spots but changed the colors in the spot pipes anchored to the bridge. The frequent alteration between scenes "in one" and full stage, accomplished by the closing of travelers, separated all equipment in the downstage into one category and everything else upstage of the close-ins in the other. The flat, bas relief monotony of the in-one segments was relieved by transparencies, gauze cut-outs and glittery applique break-up on the travelers. Highlighting on this narrow downstage ledge was confined to the arc follow spots on the stars. One device of that dear epoch is worth recalling because it was recently revived, notably in "1776." It is the use of what were called "effect spots," random, separated pin spots that the performers wandered in and out of. The coloration of all spots never varied from a three-color system of no-color pink, steel blue and special lavender, and all three were banged on together and called white for the book comedy scenes. Oh yes, there was a sumptuous deep blue to enhance the Production Numbers. The manufacture of the parabolic reflector unit that produced a strong beam brought in Backlighting, which was the first real stab at creating space and aerial haze onstage. Also, it pulled the actors away from the backgrounds, just like D. W. Griffith close-ups. So now a secondary phalanx overhead gave paths of sunlight and moonlight. The projector housing focused on the diagonal downstage took up a good two feet of hanging space—four pipes' worth equaled eight feet. As the tonnage of carpentry moving in the flys piled up, the congestion became fierce. The invention of the compact, sealed beam Par X-Rays, which replaced the bulky compartment borderlights, let in some air. A few of us who were forced to worry about the traffic problem in the air (Feder, Mielziner and Bay) independently came up with a simple discovery. The trim on the first portal of a musical is sixteen-foot minimum and on upstage portals even higher. Overhead pipes to mask hang nineteen to twenty-four feet off the deck; the hanging space between the first pipe and the first backlight pipe is less than six feet; and so on upstage. A scaled sectional view illustrates quite plainly that the angle between the regular pipe and the corresponding backlight pipe is negligible—they are both toplights. *Voila,* we eliminated the redundant sacred first pipe and the other old overhead general pipes, leaving strong warm and cool backlighting from above. (The first pipe hangs around for specials on actors or scenery.) The clusters of low-wattage bitsy boom lamps were traded in for warm and cool 1500-watt ellipsoidal cannons hung low for strong crosslight; box booms came in, and modern lighting started to take shape. In bold outline, modern lighting is a lucid pattern of paths of strong backlight, paths of strong sidelight, the necessary fill illumination from the fronts, plus specials as needed. The rich hues are confined to the backlight with pipes divided into warm and cool, which in turn are circuited right, center and left stage. Two high-wattage ellipsoidals in warm and two in cool will cover across stage from each low boom position. The box booms

135

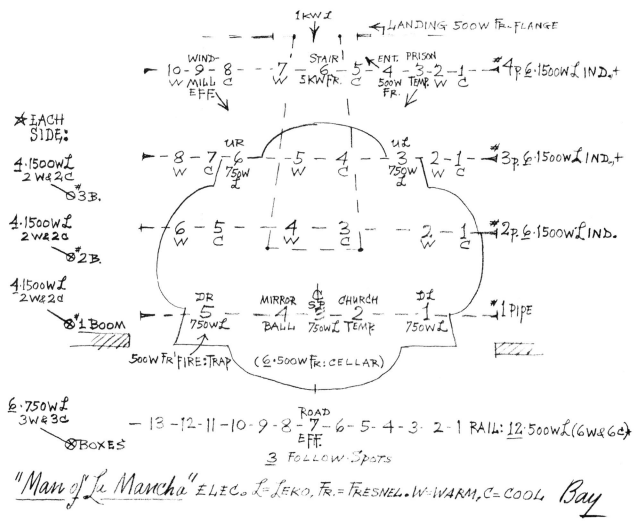

Howard Bay "Man of La Mancha" [electrics] (New York, 1965)

(always ellipsoidals) carry the side lighting out onto the apron and are colored the same as the booms. From their position on the balcony face, the rail fronts (always ellipsoidals) serve as pale washes, passive illumination brought up to the level of good visibility without canceling out the sharp modeling of the back and sides. Here also a warm and a cool have replaced the three colors. Each color may be broken up into right, center and left stage. An equipment catalog chart specifies the right lens for the length of throw.

When box sets went out of style and straight shows began to be mounted with skeletal fragments sans sides and ceilings, a ready-made lighting approach was at hand: the above outlined musical format that we had refined through the years. Perhaps a different circuiting for split sets, perhaps softer colors, perhaps a

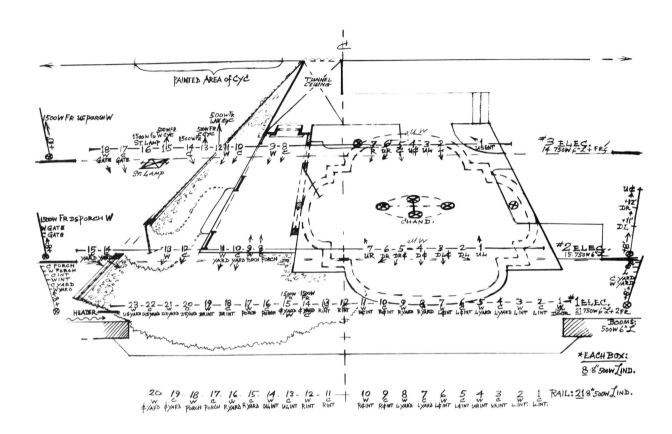

Howard Bay "Toys in the Attic" [light plot] (New York, 1960)

few specials from the rail, perhaps more pattern projections, but the ABCs of back, sides and fronts hold firm. And that is where we are in the lighting for the proscenium theatre. The puzzlement is why it took so long to junk the pile up of units from every direction, each canceling the other out, and logically build on the clear-cut three directions, their distinct functions and their meshing into a controlled figuration.

Now the steps in the design process. The first reading of the script should partake of that open-pored receptivity discussed in the chapter on scenic design. Let the playwright's words roll over you; soak in the mood, the atmosphere and all those elusive, intangible smells peculiar to this one drama. On the second reading get down to solid matter. At the top of the list are recordings of the seasons, the weather and the time of day or night. Changes during the course of action are noted, as are the Acts of God, such as thunder, lightning, rain. Specified artificial light sources are jotted down, as are any integral cues for switching fixtures on and off. All these notations are not just checked in the script but are lined up on a chart. This bill of demands from the dramatist needs fleshing out—needs An Approach, as we say in Serious Theatre Conferences. Mayhaps the director has already provided a hint, such as, I See It All Sort Of

Underwater, A Fragile Dream In The Mind's Eye of Deirdre. (You would be astonished at the number of plays that started out as dreams and ended up with three gag writers in Philadelphia.)

Or, you can stand back and brood over the theme, the main line, the spine of the script and suddenly come up with an overriding motif: enervating heat, damp clamminess, dappled sunlight through foliage, a phosphorescent glow, flickering candles with mystery in between—or maybe the feeling of being underwater. The choice must be the inevitable choice befitting the angle of the particular production, given not only the script, but the director, the company, the setting, the costumes and the audience. Before you are wafted away on the wings of your inspiration, recheck the play to determine whether any absolute script requirements run against the grain of your big concept and whether it allows freedom to underscore the dramatic development of the plot. After all, lighting is the prime visual aid that can shift and flow with the action, so don't get constipated with an inflexible grand plan.

In the expansive, euphoric early period color is fondled in the search for a talisman. Not only does every dramatic work conjure up its associative slice of the spectrum, but it can be narrowed still further by color qualities: harsh or soft, acid or subdued, vibrating or quiet, etc. This is all subjective, almost mystical talk but it cannot be brought to heel by dragging in the Science of Color. Neat and predictable lab findings are out because of the infinite variables in the absorbent and reflective surfaces and in the decidedly impure color media we use. The impure theatrical color media, impossible to correlate with the light primaries, are pale, bastard tints that transmit the maximum source light and are kind to skin tones. Also, different lamps, lenses and dimmer intensities distort color, as does dust in the air. The only insurance against total reliance on trial-and-error knowledge gathered onstage is to assemble a test room. A sizeable light, leakproof cubicle is needed with one white wall and facing it one of each instrument available, with dimmers to handle same, and samples of all color media in a handy file. The other two walls would be decorated with exhibits of lamps, lenses, cable, connectors, instrument performance charts, switchboard wiring diagrams and the spectrum. Each observer of the tests should compile his own notebook describing the resultant color shades from all the test combinations of each lamp with each color filter at different dimmer readings hitting different colored surfaces. Individual descriptions are important because color names are notoriously fuzzy and nontransferable from one observer to another. The quartz iodine bulbs throw color differently than the standard incandescents.

Color media is manufactured in gelatine, plastic and glass. Gelatine, being fugitive, bleeds out too rapidly for use in high-wattage units and has been supplanted by plastics (trade names: Roscolene and Cinemoid). The only loss has been the gelatine Special Lavender, which has not been truly matched in plastic cellophane. For strong Par X-Rays only glass holds up; glass is expensive and the color range is limited. Mylar, which is practically indestructible, is coming on the market. Don't be sold light primaries or very little light will seep out of your X-Rays.

Sheets of color are delightful playthings, but don't get carried away for two reasons. First, the right restricted palette fits the production at hand. The appropriate blues are either on the purple side or on the green side; the warms are a lurid amber, a greenish yellow, a bluish pink or a pale soft pink; or there are no obvious blues or warms but the predominant note is a special lavender or a cool white, and so on. Second, a wild assortment winds up as no color as the lamps pile up on top of each other. The geography of the three basic directions is fully exploited and clear modeling is created when the saturated, obviously hot-and-cold

Reinhart Zimmermann   "Return of Ulysses" (Copenhagen, 1969)

motivating sources are assigned to the backlight; the mild bled-out passive fill comes in from the fronts through pale no-color filters and the odd in-between values from the sides. The tough choices are the sides, because the introduction of a positive note from what are usually arbitrary and formal sources tends to detract from the backlight. As a result, more often than not the booms and boxes gravitate toward the lavender-violet-magenta family with the least saturated frames in the boxes. These tints, which are not destructive of skin tones, enrich the shadows and the depths of most fabric colors.

The separation of acting and scenic instruments is a key factor in the maneuverability of your building blocks, the lamp units. With the exception of smooth washes on cycs and drops demanding X-Rays and/or scoops, Fresnels deliver controlled accents on scenery. It is not always possible to pick the right gel for a painted surface the first time around, so a bit of experimenting may be necessary. Making up two sets of frames with a first and second choice is efficient and time-saving. The angle at which you hit plastic scenery is all-important; often two or more units in different coloring from different angles spot a built object. The ultimate appearance of scenery is unpredictable because the amount and influence of bounce and spill from the acting area lamps is hard to calculate. If there is a choice, the lighting designer opts for a dark ground covering—a light-absorbing pile carpeting is especially fine.

Color is a very elusive affair. It is in the thrall of peripheral vision, subconscious associations and fluctuating connotations. Styles change in what is considered the acceptable tints for moonlight and sunlight onstage. Once upon a time moonlight was a heady purple called Urban Blue; then for a spell, greenish blue; and now it has been calmed down to a more ambiguous lavender-steely tone. Sunlight has passed from violent orange amber, through acid lemon, tan, and for the moment a blend of pink and light-straw is deemed fitting. The recent orgy of color filters and darkroom manipulation throwing film sequences into monochromatic and psychedelic ranges loosens up our color choices in the theatre—we have greater license to splash about with artificial mixtures. Attention must be paid to fashion photography, which molds our color habits.

Page references for illustrations

Projections have been used and misused a great deal lately. Long ago it was discovered that projections are no substitute for concrete scenery. Visions in space do possess a tempting fluidity that furnishes a dynamic shift of mood without cumbersome bulk clattering across the boards. There is no escape from the magic-lantern quality of a projected image; it has a very special luminosity, a life of its own that is not of the same world as that inhabited by the actor. This shimmering ambiguity is dandy if you wish a fairyland or an extra comment superimposed on the solid playing area. And projections divide into two classifications: the color organ recital saturated with atmosphere and the separate graphic data addressed directly to the audience. The subjective, symbolic, impressionist, abstract wing drives toward a total stage universe of translucent cycs, gauzes, and imperceptible layers washed by units upstage, on bridges, crossing from towers, from the boxes, the balcony rail and the booth. If the director and the designer wield sufficient muscle they hang a gauze from proscenium to proscenium in front of the pin-spotted performers. From the floating platter at Bayreuth, Von Karajan's Wagner at Salzburg, to Von Karajan and Schneider-Siemssen's *Tristan and Isolde* at the Met, Nirvana is the immersion of the singers in a fluctuating kaleidoscope that extends the musical score in visual terms. Joseph Svoboda has veered away from his hard-edge screen shapes to crumpled mesh and two-way mirrors that blur definition and dislocate the geography of the stage volume.

140
142
143

The critical, documentary projection makes no pretense of absorbing the actors into its orbit. It is a parallel or counterpoint thematic expansion in pictures of the action. From Meyerhold to Piscator, Brecht, the Living Newspaper, Svoboda's *The Soldiers*, the frank separation of editorial graphics and performing arena tends toward stylistic eclecticism and a technical simplicity of sharp images (both film and still) and precise screen boundaries.

We in the U.S. are tardy in handling projections beyond Linnebach blobs and childish leaf gobos in spotlights. There is a simple explanation for our retardation; we have no state theatres, no permanent homes where experimentation is a natural adjunct to the onward and upward march of theatrical art. Our commercial playhouses differ radically, bookings are uncertain, and backstages are so cramped that it is risky to lean on projected images because the widest-angle lenses are unable to throw a sizable picture without distortion from variable, short-range hanging positions. And it doesn't help that primitive mechanization is confined to low-wattage instruments; Broadway managers are reluctant to assume the wages of operators to change glass slides—with costs what they are. The gypsy in a loft with a home carousel, some dishes with dyes plus oil plus water sloshed around may be delicious hobbycraft, but it is a mite primitive for contemporary theatrical projections. It just won't make it, you know, man; Fillmore East went away centuries ago. Our stagelighting firms are lagging behind the lamp manufacturers and the lens grinders. Not

Reutenward "Faust" (Stockholm, 1969)

only the aesthetic development of projections emanate from the Central European opera houses and repertory companies but they have sparked the engineering of modern hardware. Both Pani of Vienna and Reich and Vogel of Berlin turn out 5-kilowatt and 10-kilowatt incandescent and high-powered Zenon housings (Kliegl Bros., U.S. agents). They are not cheap, delivery is not by return mail, and parts are not available at your supermarket—Plan Ahead. Plastic frosted and semitransparent screens are distributed by Raven Screen, New York.

Ideally, with all the leisure in the world, the light plot would not be poured in concrete until after the lighting designer has observed a run-through of the play. This leisure does not exist, because a run-through seldom transpires earlier than a week before setup in the theatre and the equipment is in the last lap of assembly in the shop. So, the light plot must be constructed on the devoted perusal of the script plus production conferences with the director, the stage manager and the other designers. The lighting department must cultivate a skeptical stance at these gab fests because there is nothing quite like the subject of stage lighting to unleash the fanciful verbiage in people—particularly in those who don't deal in amperes, cables and metal cans with bulbs in them. Separating the wheat from the chaff, so to speak, takes practice, but if one sticks close to the stage manager at least the practical requirements and rehearsal changes are known quantities. Study the scenic working drawings and the costume plates. On tracings over the master hanging plan and the section, the light plot takes form. Equipment makers furnish one-half-inch-scale templates of light housings. First pencil in the general directional coverage, then the acting specials, then take care of scenery, then marginal items for backings and effects. In every location add a few safety units for emergencies, such as the inevitable renovations in the show, for the cardinal sin is to hang a light with

Josef Svoboda   "Insect Play"   (Prague, 1965)

143

the actors standing around. In spacing units allow for swiveling and for focusing. Occasionally in crowded places lamps must be swung out on short extension arms off the pipes or booms to clear the regular hangings. Strive to avoid roving castered units that must be set, focused and struck by operators. In the commercial framework operators cost money and in noncommercial situations it is risky to depend on a body finding the precise marks and focus performance after performance.

If after a session of head scratching and futile gestures with the scale ruler you can't seem to illuminate the stage because logical positions are blocked by the set, perhaps the set has to give. For the Sacred Texts say: It Does Not Exist Until Light Reveals It, Leviticas (Sam) XXII, 12. This is the juncture, I fear, when a few words must be delivered on the Alarming Increase in splitting set design and lighting design into two jobs handled by two people. The few words are: It ain't natural. I would find it difficult not to conceive of the set and lighting simultaneously, and it would be time-consuming and inefficient to negotiate with another brain on one-half of an indivisible creative process. More departmentalization in theatre leads to more timidity and conservatism. I can think of only two exceptions to the set-lighting unity. One is in a permanent company where sundry set designers are jobbed in, but a constant light format needs minimum revamping for each presentation. Example: Jean Rosenthal's admirable ballet hookups, which even appear sparkling when no set is there. The other rational exception is the case of the set designer who is temperamentally ill-suited to cope with the rigorous organization and pressures of lighting rehearsals. Under coping will be many moments when a local brother has just dropped the last 5-kilowatt bulb (list price $65), or the wife of the star's agent flounces over with "I do think that pink is too intense, don't you?" A parting thought on the lighting specialist: exhibitionism must rear its smiling head if your career rests solely on whether or not those light rays are noticed or whether that gauze transformation is admired by the daily press.

The obvious superiority of using the three-directional general coverage with added specials is evident when applied to multi-scened ventures. Since the entire stage is blanketed from every direction with both warm and cool, the specials are truly specials and perform precise jobs for individual scenes. To punch through the general level, the specials are of high wattage—say, a 3-kilowatt Fresnel in a color peculiar to the scene. The 5-kilowatt Fresnels are coming into general usage and are saved for the grand slam when a real flood of something new and dazzling is called for. No doubt tomorrow the 10-kilowatt Fresnel will be purloined from the movies. To descent to the other end of the artillery range, the 100-watt miniature Fresnels can be hidden within the set for close-up accents.

The amount of data drawn on the plot differs in commercial and noncommercial situations. Taking Broadway productions first: the instruments, their hanging positions and colors, whether they are to be controlled individually or which groups are to be ganged together is the extent of the information presented to the production electricians at the first meeting. Broadway designers are spoiled rotten by the first-class production electricians and driven to hard liquor by the few bad ones. The electrician carries away the print; breaks it down into an instrument list, cable lengths, plugging boxes, lamps, a color order; and, most importantly, figures out the switchboards. After juggling the switchboards around, the electrician may come back to the designer with suggestions. These suggestions pertain to holding the boards down to an economical operational total. Can't these be ganged together? Do we have time to replug this bunch to save

FIX.	ST. LAMP AUX 1		US LAMP AUX 2		CHAND. AUX 4	L. LAMP AUX 3

3RD BOOM | 1500W FR W811 | US PORCH 91 | | all colors: ROSCOLENE

| #3 P. | 18 W811 GATE 83 | 17 c856 GATE 84 | 16 1500WFR W805/805 ST.LAMP 90 | 15 500WFR W811 87 | 14 c856 US CYC 89 | 13 BL CYC 86 | 12 c LAV 842½ 85 | 11 W 811 69 | 10 c 856 70 | 9 811 PORCH 54 | 8 856 PORCH 55 | 7 W R 37 | 6 W UR 36 | 5 W ¢ 35 | 4 W U¢ 34 | 3 W UL 33 | 2 W L 32 | 1 W US ENT. 31 |

2ND BOOM | 1500W FR W811/811 PORCH 88 | | GATE 2 W811/811 75 | GATE 1 c856 76 | | U¢ LAV. 3 45 | DR LAV. 2 44 | DL LAV. 842 1 43 |

| #2 P. | 15 W811 YARD 81 | 14 c856 YARD 82 | 13 W811 R.YARD 79 | 12 c856 R.YARD 80 | 11 W811 YARD 77 | 10 c856 YARD 78 | 9 W PORCH 52 | 8 c PORCH 53 | 7 W UR 30 | 6 W DR 29 | 5 W DR¢ 28 | 4 W D¢ 27 | 3 W DL¢ 26 | 2 W DL 25 | 1 W UL 24 |

1ST BOOM | 842/856 6 PORCH 51 | W811 5 PORCH 50 | W 4 INT. 42 | W 3 INT. 41 | 842/856 2 YARD 94 | W811 1 YARD 73 | | RLAV 5 40 | ¢LAV 4 39 | L.LAV842 3 38 | YARD 2 72 | YARD 1 71 | |

| #1 P. | 23 W811 US YARD 67 | 22 c856 US YARD 68 | 21 W811 DR YARD 65 | 20 c856 DR YARD 66 | 19 W DR INT 18 | 18 c DR INT 23 | 17 W811 PORCH 48 | 16 c856 PORCH 49 | 15 1500W FR W811 YARD 92 | 14 1500WFR c856 4 YARD 93 | 13 W R. INT 17 | 12 c R INT 22 | 11 W R¢ INT 16 | 10 c R¢ INT 21 | 9 W R YARD 63 | 8 c R YARD 64 | 7 W L¢ INT 15 | 6 c L¢ INT 20 | 5 ¢ L YARD 61 | 4 ¢ L YARD 62 | 3 W L INT 14 | 2 c L INT 19 | 1 W INT DOOR 13 |

RAIL 20W | 19 c 4 YARD 59 | 18 W YARD 60 | 17 c PORCH 46 | 16 W PORCH 47 | 15 c R.YARD 58 | 14 W UL INT 7 | 13 c UL INT 6 | 12 W UL INT 13 | 11 c R INT 5 | 10 W R INT 12 | 9 c R¢ INT 4 | 8 c R¢ INT 11 | 7 c L YARD 56 | 6 c L YARD 57 | 5 c L¢ INT 3 | 4 c L¢ INT 10 | 3 c UR INT 2 | W825 2 805 UR INT 9 | c842 1 851 L INT 1 | L INT. 8 |

Howard Bay "Toys in the Attic" [code layout] (New York, 1960)

dimmers? Can these 1000 watts be traded in for 750 watts, because we have some 750-watt plates open? The designer must know exactly how much to compromise without sacrificing the flexibility of the layout. The business manager may be happy that a board has been cut, but the manager doesn't have to answer the director when said director wants to know why he can't have a light right over there. When it is all straightened out the electrician will deliver a board schedule and you will enter the switch numbers next to the units and your layout is finished and sent to the blueprinter. Piano boards will be covered in the appendix.

The proscenium attack holds for the open stage with some exceptions: (1) Low angles are *verboten* because the customers on the opposite side are blinded. (2) A symmetrical layout ensures a uniform picture from all sides. The necessity of balancing off the coverage naturally limits and subdues the contrasts and the colors used with specials confined to strong downlights. Because the backlight for the north bloc of audience is the front illumination for the south bloc, it follows that proper balance depends on individual board control of every single lamp—paths of light are out and a checkerboard break-up is standard. With several units aimed at each sector of the platform the spill is widespread and beyond control. So pattern projections can add interest and variety to the diffused, arbitrary pools on the floor and on the set pieces and properties.

In the noncommercial world the designer may be stuck with many of the chores the Broadway production electrician handles. If the lighting designer is ensconced in a semi-permanent home, such as a resident company, stock or school, several locations, mainly front of the house, may be refocused or regelled, but the installation remains fairly stable.

Most schools have the edge on commercial playhouses in front-of-the-house positions with either or both ceiling beams and side slots. Ceiling beams provide a logical angle for apron and downstage areas without spill upstage on scenery, and the slots equal the makeshift box booms of the conventional houses. Ceiling beams can be considered an extension of the overhead coverage and color, with the color less saturated than the units hung backstage. Backstage pipes, booms, cable lengths, and plugging boxes must be listed and the board hookup routed.

Lighting folk accumulate too many pieces of paper. Frustrated engineers unable to find an excuse for flashing a slide rule, they make up for it with complicated documents. This pseudo-organization leads to chaos at dress rehearsal time. With a full complement of actors, singers, dancers, musicians and stagehands in suspended animation, the light designer amidst his squawk box, headphones, and little beaver assistants with containers of coffee, is scrambling between blueprints, board diagrams, focusing charts, clipboards and cue sheets struggling to find one light and match it up with the one switch that turns it on and off. This gory predicament can be avoided by lettering all the relevant material on one thing, namely the plot. After the show is focused even the unwieldy plot can be transposed to a simple code on a piece of cardboard that folds into the pocket (with cues listed on the reverse side). Extreme example: the original *Man of La Mancha* plot was confined to one 3 x 5 inch index card—one side of the card, of course. That is just a different fetish, isn't it?

But we are jumping ahead. While the hardware is being assembled in the shop, two tasks are as yet undone: cues and fixtures. The stage manager has noted the obvious, mandatory cues; a sensitive, close study of rehearsals will trigger the subtle changes in atmosphere and emphasis that make lighting a positive contribution to a play's unraveling on the stage. Although it is a bloody truism in any art endeavor: work backwards, hold the fireworks for the end, don't run out of variety—in short, orchestrate the illumination. Save that 5-kilowatt Fresnel for the denouement with our anti-hero naked center stage, sardonically awaiting the Bomb to be popped by a CIA code clerk, a transvestite high on astrology and pretty buttons.

The timing of the cues can be calculated at the last run-through before moving into the theatre. Fixtures must be chosen carefully because they tend to shrink when mounted on the set. The outsized value of everything onstage must be matched by the importance of the visible light sources that are the rationale for those terrific blasts of illumination from off-stage. The hanging of chandeliers is tricky on two counts: (1) they are scene stealers and (2) they are apt to foul up the light rays aimed at the acting area. Everything powered by electricity falls within the domain of the electrical department. This goes for all mechanization of wagons, turntables, etc., and naturally covers sound. This impinges on the lighting designer insofar as he must be aware of help doubling between board cues, sound cues, and scene-shifting controls.

The last production conference before moving out of the shop is the crucial one that coordinates all the diverse physical elements and guarantees a smooth opening. The production carpenter and the electrician decide the order of hanging, and with the prop man distribute all floor storage and movements. The lighting designer enters the debate at the point that the stage manager inquires when the acting company can get onstage. That is the big question, and your estimation had better be accurate. The director, through the stage manager, pressures for an early company call, but if you are not ready the whole procedure comes unstuck—not only in a physical sense, but company morale melts away if ladder work and focusing bog down run-throughs. There is never enough time to light a show in that squeezed slot between the carpenter handing over the reins and the troubadors pouring through the stage door. Madness holds sway if the actors take over before all units are hung and focused and colored and plugged into the boards, the communication system has been placed in the middle of the house, and the designer from this vantage point has run through and checked all the circuits. But it is not a disaster if there has not been time to set levels and cues because costumes and make-up alter levels, and an alert, prepared lighting designer can set up levels and cues during the run-through without stopping the action—except during the few rough moments when several cues pile up and the board men can't write fast enough.

Backtracking to focusing time, some overlapping of scenery, hanging and focusing eases the schedule. Front-of-the-house units can be polished off without killing the carpenters' work-light upstage. Actually, after a little practice you don't require inky blackness to focus any spotlight, and with more practice matters can be further expedited by putting two men in different locations, for instance on opposite booms, and shuttling back and forth. If you have done your homework and know where every lamp goes and why, focusing should breeze along. Check off every circuit and its switch on your plot as it is focused, and at the end of focusing transpose your layout to the condensed code sheet mentioned earlier. On deportment at dress rehearsals: actors are extra-vulnerable during these exhausting times, so carefully shunt work that can be done tomorrow morning with only the crew about to tomorrow morning. At the same time you must firmly stop rehearsal to allow the board men to catch up on writing out a cue, because if lights fall behind the rehearsal is a waste technically.

Before reading Ralph Holmes's indispensable appendix on control systems an introductory remark is in order here. The physical plant and gadgetry craze rampant in educational theatre has one unfortunate result in the lighting department. Too often the very latest in electronic systems have been installed, thereby by-passing an essential learning step, the old reliable piano boards. Not only do the piano boards simply demonstrate the routing of electricity from instrument to switch and dimmer, but the commercial theatre and less fortunate school and regional theatres have nothing but piano boards. The student who has been punching all those complicated buttons on a quarter-of-a-million-dollar console throughout his formative years is going to feel rather naked when he confronts a battered piano board out there in real life.

VI.
In The Theatre

The special lines for scenery and lights are spotted and run in ahead of the show. The production carpenter handles this job with the help of the house troops. The running of the spot lines is dictated by the latest revised edition of the hanging plot worked out at the final conference of the designer and the production heads.

Since the railroads have gone to seed, enterprising transfer lines have tailored vans for hauling shows overland. We bid adieu to the Romance of the Rails, which consisted of chasing lost baggage cars through the dusty network of indifferent dispatchers and expediters (I love that word). So the trucks drive right up to the loading door more or less on schedule, and the deceptively slack-looking ceremony of putting on a show starts grinding.

The day of reckoning is the load-in, the big payoff for slaving over a hot drawing board; wheedling vendors into impossible delivery dates; stopping the upholsterers from adding tasteful touches; slyly sidetracking competitor shows in the electrical factory by collaring the few decent lamps; tracking down an itinerant magician to conjure up a contraption that dances, lights up, waves the American flag and explodes; paying one's respects to the period frails who traffic in antiques; dissipating endless hours listening to the

Business Manager lecture on the deteriorating state of the economy. These sessions come to a close when the Manager is picked up in his Lincoln Continental by his spouse in a Maximilian fur wrap. Add to that contacting the choreographer on a lily pad at the far end of Fire Island about the breakaway bleachers in the Forum scene and laying out a sizable sum in saloons to forestall the electrician from taking that rosier job with Hal Prince.

This moment of truth, the load-in, reveals the efficiency of the production crew and the quality of the shop job. In healthier times when there were knowing, stable managements with staffs attached, production heads were integral parts of the staff. That gave them independence from the shops, and they would worry and shout and carry on and make jolly well sure that everything was finished before it left the shops. In a disquieting changeover, the shops now assign the head carpenter, whose allegiance naturally remains with the shop. What is truly maddening is that the shops leave a lot of loose ends to patch up in the theatre, and then commando battalions swarm in loaded with hardware disrupting the normal procedure of putting on a show. And their carpenter agent idles along on the sidelines of the chaos.

The question of whether to hang the scenery or the electrics first should be decided on the merits of each case. Once there was no doubt: the Property Master laid the ground cloth, the carpenter hung his ceiling and his portal, his flats were jogged around and fastened to each other, and the ceiling was lowered into place. Meanwhile, out of harm's way, the electrician over in the corner hooked up his boards, then attached his balcony pans and ran cable out front to light up the lamps in these pans. Because the set had already been completed, the electrician was permitted to hang his first pipe and any upstage equipment and flange or just place backing units and wire his practicals. Props dressed the set as dictated by the designer, the stage manager diddled with his control desk, and the hired help began to seep outdoors to the alehouse. At this juncture, with the sadistic worklight denigrating everything onstage, the director made his entrance, stomped down the aisle and rasped, "How could you dream up those godforsaken drapes? I am going to my hotel and when I return—" All in all, those were idyllic times.

The popularity of the unit set on the open stage, with high trims for the overhead maskings and the lights even higher behind these borders, discourages the hanging of masking and pipes after the set has been erected. Where you have a large structure permanently planted onstage, hanging the electrics must come first. There must be sufficient space next to the pipes to allow for the bridges needed in focusing the units, because there is no place to plant A-ladders to reach the lamps. If there is only a limited cluster of lamps that cannot be approached, a bo's'n chair on a traveller track covers much territory, but it is no substitute for a bridge in terms of regard for life and limb.

Obviously, an overall deck should be laid before the stage becomes cluttered with anything—scenery, lights or props. Everything that hangs should be flown out before floor elements are assembled. In fact, the ideal course is to load the trucks with thought given to what is disgorged first; then you can hold the floor-handled scenery and the props on the trucks until needed. Expert crew heads lay out the work so that (1) things are handled once and not moved from here to there and back again—none of that where in the hell did some idiot hide those stretchers? (2) The men are separated into teams that function simultaneously upstage, downstage, offstage and up in the flys. The telltale sign of a low-grade road carpenter is the frozen landscape of scores of bodies observing one of their number tying a knot.

A footnote about those teams carrying on all over the place; they don't perform unless each gang is supervised by someone familiar with the show. It is bad economics to carry less than the maximum road crew allowed by the I.A. contract, because one road man not only can do the labor of at least three locals but also he can see to it that the transient help is gainfully employed. With the road well-nigh nonexistent, the help—with the exception of the New Haven boys and a few survivors spread thinly across the map—is plain depressing.

Because backstage real estate is always so constricted, it helps to banish the props to the front of the house for a while. Unpacked and tenderly distributed on tarpaulins, the stuff won't spoil the motheaten seats and carpeting of the emporium, and the hand props come in handy for rehearsals in the lounge. This may seem to be the spot to discuss rigging, but since it falls within the carpenter's domain, consult Appendix I, Stage Machinery.

For information about actual lighting, see the chapter on lighting. Here we deal with departmental coordination, which is a pleasant way of saying that the designer is the referee who prevents the carpenter and the electrician from throttling each other. The prop man is an outcast, who may be heard muttering, "Nobody gives me a chance to work. If Mister McClintic were still alive . . . ." It behooves the designer to shuttle scenery assembly so that focusing can continue through it all. That calls for a little planning, such as where every lamp hits on the bare floor; the luxury of awaiting the completed picture and absolute darkness would, of course, provide more comfort, but it would cost monies. This sort of ad-lib dovetailing of lumber and electricity is one more reason that scenery-and-lighting design should be wrapped up in a single artist. The designer can't do a thing about the larger foolishness (plunging into rehearsal with an embryonic script, casting a TV face and body as an actress, etc.) but he can retard the Spiraling Production Costs by having his assistant focus one boom while he is focusing another. He can insist that that set piece be assembled off in the corner by the light of a strong torch rather than center stage in all the worklights. A truly sizable saving accrues from the tenacious push to get everything hung, assembled and in working order before the company descends onstage. Once the Equity members are loose the costs are compounded—and with the pit band squatting down there, the backers' ill-gotten gains really melt away—all those high-priced people watching a brother change a colored gelatine.

All that needs to be said about dressing the set is that it, too, must reflect forethought and an eye for speed in mounting. Under forethought: necessary adaptations of props must be performed in the shop. It is more economical to build the right thing than to fool with a store-bought number that is not quite what you have in mind. Scale and what fits into the ensemble is a far tougher problem in furnishings than in scenery because the designer must choose furnishings piece by piece with no surety of compatibility until the fatal day in the theatre. If you have gnawing doubts, drag along an alternative—a returnable alternative, that is.

In the course of the setup the prop man must lie in wait and pounce at the off moment when the carpenter and the juice have finished something and are looking the other way. Items permanently attached to the set come first, then anchoring the bric-a-brac (with wire and mortician's wax), and then placing the furniture and making temporary marks that are shifted one inch by the director as a matter of principle. The absolutely crazy collection of tools, appliances and oddments that spills out of the prop box is the insurance that spells undisturbed, ongoing tech rehearsals. The prop man is a busy housekeeper, stacking and unpacking and lining up everything in the sequence of its use in the running order.

The young designer should have noted between the lines that the designer is in charge of the activity of making ready for the acting troupe. There really is no one else. At any particular point in time there is one person in command. When the thespians descend, it is the director who is in charge, and the designer in his subsidiary role makes life comfortable for the director and company. When there are audiences out there the stage manager is absolute tyrant, otherwise the proceedings come unstuck. Prior to the time the company tumbles onstage the designer must be a resilient but tough diplomat who propels all departments toward a cohesive physical production. Not many seasons will come and go before the novice designer wakes up to the cynical thought that most managers are great negative critics. They are up on the grosses in L.A., where to eat in Detroit, who supplanted who in Myra Morningstar's sack, and so forth, but are of little aid in putting on a show and a decided deterrent to the creative process of doing something a little different—even in the commercial ball park. Brush aside the highly debatable proposition that the designer is a talented dreamer that requires the sober ministrations of the manager, that realist who contributed several large bills to ponies yesterday, and nothing has changed if the nags have died and we have a wide tie and sideburns and dialogue about putting a rock band smack *onstage!* Crazy, huh?

After all the pushing and pulling, checking the changes, finishing the focusing and running through the circuits here we are at the first tech rehearsal—with not a moment to spare. The purpose of this occasion is to familiarize the cast with the sets, with the entrances and exits, with the props and any mechanical novelties they may be called upon to deal with in the action. This is not the time for words as we skip from cut to cue. Our alert designer is poised at his squawk box centrally located on the orchestra floor where he is hooked up with the stage manager, the switchboards, and front follow-spot operators if they exist. If of nimble mind, the designer can rough in levels and cues without halting the rehearsal. Also he can relay orders to the carpenter and props through the stage manager. The director usually has a P.A. mike independent of the designer's system so that he can move out of earshot of the infernal murmuring.

The first tech runthrough is a psychological watershed whose pivotal importance is never sensed while happening because everyone is submerged in a legion of messy details. It is the critical moment in the saga of a production when the ultimate shape and rhythm of a show is made visible or disintegration infects the organism. The citizens out there are dumfounded by reports that many theatrical ventures actually get worse in the course of tryouts. Constructive impetus hinges on father-figure director grasping the helm, inspiring the troops and squashing the disrupters in the shape of producer's wives, agents, analysts and sundry vultures. If you ever wondered about the origins of the lament that there are no straight men any more, you have never been engulfed in the retinue of authorities that mill around a show in the making.

Although Papa Director is All, the designer can do his bit for the morale and the general uplift in these trying times, not only by behaving sharp and bushy-tailed but by identifying with the long-term aims of the director and pushing toward their coming to pass. Egos must be filed under Home Use Only. Diligent note-taking postpones corrections that need not occupy the whole company but can be tidied up tomorrow morning with only the stagehands present. When midnight rolls around and everyone expires, it devolves on you to lay out with the crew hands the calls and the work priorities for the morrow. Leave the number of men to be called to the discretion of the heads; they not only know best but there are only four hours between 8 a.m. and noon, and the company returns at one and everyone eats lunch.

Make-up is seldom required until dress, but for obvious reasons it is nice to have the right clothes worn at tech. It is curious that tons of scenery always get delivered on the right date but the costume house has trouble finishing all the articles of wardrobe specified in the contract. Thyroid gnomes are always flying in, trailing pieces of apparel and cartons of trimming.

If the schedule is tight, which it invariably is, the scenic touch-up may need to be performed some midnight. You must give ample notice to the scenic shop and arrange suitable work light through the grumpy offices of the house electrician. And you keep your brothers company through the night.

By definition dress rehearsal is a duplicate of the performance offered to the opening night customers. (I read it in some textbook on the theatre.) Actually, dress rehearsals are stop-and-start affairs, with bugs ironed out before passing on. If all and sundry have done their chores and a unified spirit pervades the playhouse, the pieces should mesh without hysteria. In your domain falls the organization of the changes and the routining of the boards for the wilder cues. The cues and their timing must be recorded by the stage manager.

Without fail some forgotten particle fouls up the occasion—not necessarily a child actor or an animal. It is simpler and faster to change a few acres of scenery than one corset. Directors and designers must make instant and brutal decisions, murdering their most adored creations if they constipate the tempo and progression of the drama. A concentrated, transient snippet of business may replace a cumbersome expository scene and its attendant scenic effects. At dress rehearsal it is revealed to the designer whether he has painted himself into a corner with a rigid format that discourages script and directorial renovations. What is important and what is unimportant become crystal clear as all elements swing along in unison for the first time. The worthy director immediately plots how to bring the big changes to pass, and leaves crooked hemlines to trusty subordinates. The smell of death is in the air if the brass becomes all sweaty about crooked hemlines. The young designer will be less likely to slit his wrists and bring a promising career to an untimely end if he cultivates an objectivity concerning criticism. If you are hunched over your squawk box vainly trying to untangle cue 36B before the actors are in cue 38C and the producer leans over and hisses how in the hell can we have a show with that horrendous backdrop, pause and consider: (1) The drop may be ghastly and may have to be traded in for a more suitable hanging. (2) When life is awry it is difficult to pinpoint the defects in elusive intangibles, such as words and music (and wooden Indians with run-of-the-play contracts), so sets, costumes and lights are the visible, concrete targets that attract frustrations that have no other handy outlets. Chained in a dusty theatre for eternities of rehearsals, previews, performances and gabfests, even the designer can learn to loathe his own brain child mutely crouched up there.

Anecdotes about the mad, mad doings at dress rehearsals stretch from here to there, but the designer need hold tight to only one small observation: When the smoke clears nothing matters but a clean, zestful out-of-town opening and a clear understanding of the revisions for the Broadway opening. That statement may seem an unnecessarily moronic bromide, but wait until you have been there. The dream world of the Ritz in Boston and the Barclay in Philadelphia is way beyond Fellini—get Abbott, get Bob Fosse, where for godsakes is Mike Nichols? Simon must have a phone, what's that writer freak who did the undress Goldilocks? What do you think jets are for, *paison*? These lively gatherings of the production staff, augmented by attorneys, relatives, reformed hoods, and well-wishing competitors of the management, are obligatory social events. In the confusion of the festivities the designer is often mistaken for the playwright and is chided for creating such an expensive production with so many scenes.

Even though it may be desperately sandwiched in on opening day, one nonstop runthrough preceding the opening is mandatory. If the designer and the crew must forego a well-earned night's slumber to guarantee that it will come off as a non-stop event, so be it. Don't give credence to the view that this little old out-of-town opening really isn't important, it's more in the nature of a dress rehearsal, you know. The critics are there, the locusts from New York are there, the word of mouth starts fanning out throughout the length and breadth of the eastern seaboard, and an atmosphere is born. This goes double for shows that are first exposed to one of those scintillating preview crowds. (There must be another way to say word of mouth.)

Actual work time in the tryout stretch is a bit less than the calendar indicates. Performances knock out the evenings and the two matinee afternoons. Add to that the Equity day off, picture calls, TV and other press chores, replacement and understudy rehearsals, preparations for moving, and so on. Rewrites, restaging, and rerouting keep the cue sheets and the prop list rather active. In fact, rerouting may call for extensive rehanging and even rebuilding. The limited number of basic mechanical layouts is not all tradition and inertia, for these layouts do allow maximum reshuffling with a minimum expenditure of time and labor. Not that you must hew to the tried and true, but you do have to anticipate possible changes in any departures from the standard. What was conceived as a lavish full-stage scene may be shrunk to a perfunctory crossover bit or vice versa. The attendant revamping, rehanging and rerouting on the floor must be both possible and capable of being handled with ease and speed, and is one of the prime reasons for the overall deck, in which a new guide can be scored with a power saw in minutes.

Stagehands need rehearsal, just like actors, and they need several shows without wholesale changes, to deliver smooth performances. The amount of changes that you hand to the crews must be carefully calculated and timed. Anything that can be cleaned up through notes is swell, but you must gauge the point where notes fail and schedule a rehearsal. Crew calls cost money, so hold off until a healthy chunk of work can be polished off in one fell swoop. Tryouts are debilitating, to put it gently, and since you are the custodian of backstage morale among the laboring classes (often counteracting managerial insensitivity), husbanding the crew's strength and spirits is rather important.

While valiantly struggling for time to carry out departmental tasks, do not mislay the reason you and everyone else are on hand: to assist the director in hammering out a dazzling piece of theatre.

Free of the clammy, driven competitiveness and the everlasting starting-from-scratch waste of the commercial scene, the resident or college outfit can calmly plan in its own home on a base of accumulated experience and materials. Wagons, motors, steps, flats, doors and windows are filed away. Switchboards, masking, eyes, gauzes, and front-of-the-house lights are there, and one can focus on items unique to a production. The danger lies in drifting into superimposing a single unvarying format on all and assorted dramas. We shall refrain from mentioning the nefarious practice in academic circles whereby the instructor hogs all the design assignments on the mealy rationale that the students learn from the precepts of their superiors. What must be mentioned is that it devolves on the designers and the director to strive to approximate the spirit and rhythm of professional onstage rehearsals within the diluted tempo of the school calendar. Untrained actors have not developed an immunity to falling sandbags or erratic switchboard behavior; they need to put mechanical matters behind them and ease into peaceful runthroughs devoted only to performance. Temperament and shouting and containers of coffee and dragging into the wee hours is not show business, it is nonsense.

VII.
Economics of The Craft

Before prudent parental advice is waived aside and theatrical design is pursued as one's chosen career, there are certain nasty statistics that cannot be whisked under the rug. At this juncture in the annals of the stage perhaps half a dozen scenic designers squeeze a respectable living out of Broadway, and you may have noticed the relentlessly declining total of productions from season to season. There is no sure palliative for the economic straits of our so-called glamour profession. Our union is the United Scenic Artists of America, Local 829, affiliated with the Brotherhood of Painters, Decorators and Paperhangers of the U.S. and Canada, AFL-CIO. Local 829 exercises jurisdiction over the eastern third of the country's scenic, lighting and costume designers; film and television art directors; scenic artists in theatre, film and TV; costume stylists; mural artists; and diorama and display workers. The various contracts set modest fees and wage scales, humane working conditions, and are free of muscle for hiring minimum crews or other feather-bedding devices. A demerit must be handed the union for its failure to hammer out an apprentice system. Speaking from the tired vantage point of seventeen years as president of the quixotic, talent-packed club, I would say that we have been too ladylike to the sharks that infest the entertainment waters; too conscious of being artists about it all. Beyond the usual theatre larceny the designer is really short-changed when the

"London After Midnight"
[film]   (1927)

pie is cut. Overlooking the killer that the designer is hired as a temporary employee while staggering under the costs of running a business (office-studio, phones, answering service, expensive help, research, materials, heavy entertaining, etc.), it is the payoff that never comes that hurts. A hit returns more take-home dollars to the assistant stage managers than it does to the creators of the sets, costumes and lights. The individually negotiated weekly pittance all of a sudden is dubbed a royalty just like the comfortable authors' percentages when the day comes that the box office falls off and the royalty crowd are asked to take a cut. P.S.: The designers do not share in film, stock, records—any subsidiary rights—and more often than not receive nothing from foreign reproductions that pirate their sketches and plans. The Dramatists' Guild, which wields the only leverage abroad, couldn't care less. Speaking of barracudas, wait until you are introduced to the better grade West End managerial gentry; the Mittle Europa breed you know about.

These gloomy particulars are by way of hinting that one must plan to supplement the income derived from legitimate theatre design. The diversification channels are film and television art direction, industrial shows, exhibitions, trade fairs and interior design. In short, areas that cry out for theatrics on top of graphic talent. Dramatic designers do not fare so well where the sketch is the end product rather than a promise. Do not enter the lists against the legions ground out by Pratt, Parsons, Cooper Union and the Rhode Island School of Design. You have the edge over these bland tradesmen in the infusion of emotional juices and dramatic fireworks. The spirit of the carnival is mighty handy in pushing certain items.

As you know, we no longer speak of the Film Industry. In the historical archives you will uncover descriptions of Hollywood art departments which were service departments in every sense of the phrase.

Laid out with art directors, assistant art directors, set designers (not in the theatrical sense but as drafts-men), technical follow-up men, model makers, an art director in charge of the drafting room, sketch artists, files of all stock units, an art director in charge of the stock files, blueprint machinery, secretaries, and a Supervising Art Director who reported to the Production Office when he wanted to go to the bathroom. Underneath the Disneyland syrup, in the drafting rooms, in the shops and on the backlots labored the greatest concentration of skilled artisans in the history of the world. There is no point in dwelling on the thought because they were rarely used to full potential and they are now scattered to the four winds. The blacklist rearing its lovely head in '47 was the beginning of the end. The poison that infected that company town spread far beyond the statistical total of blacklisted craftsmen.

Anyway, the book is closed on the studio-manufactured film that was designed and executed in every detail from a single stylistic approach. It was an honorable history stretching from the Menzies-Fairbanks Senior team, through the great German architect-designers of the '20s and early '30s, the Grots and Dreirs and Ushers and Days of Hollywood, to the Rank empire's Alfred Junge and the Vincent Korda historical splurges. The last stand was Wakewitch and Trauner. It was a hothouse species that cannot thrive in the second half of the twentieth century.

For the last remaining super sets, such as *Dolly* and *The Andromeda Strain,* technicians have been scraped together from all the studios because the luxury of full staffs on yearly guarantees is long gone. A few independent special effects outfits manage to survive and cater to films and TV on a one-shot subcon-

"Great Expectations"
[film] (1947)

George Wakewitch "Leather Nose" [film] (1951)

tract basis. The multitude of craft locals of the International Alliance of Theatre and Stage Employees that control Hollywood appear unduly numerous, but in the main they are the logical breakdown into the specialties needed to put together a motion picture. Local 829 has a working relationship with the coast art directors and scenic artists.

You may be rather lonely in East Coast filmmaking. No one, but no one, keeps anybody on the payroll beyond some front-office dressing. You are engaged late as an art director, and you pick it up from there and put it together. Perhaps there is a production manager ahead of you, but you would do well to screen his cronies before accepting them as your crew heads—although in Manhattan, they are outfitted in sport gear as if they had just dropped in from the Beverly Hills pool. In the microcosm known as East Coast film production the stunner is the category labeled set dressing. This is a gambit of the union to plant two expensive prop men on a picture. You can do nothing about this ploy, but you must be thoroughly unpopular by insisting on choosing the furnishings—the high-priced prop-dresser must tag along and scribble out requisitions. All in all you need not be awed by what the old hands assure you is the time-honored way to do things. Except for the cameramen, a few carpenters and maverick grips left over from the circus, it is a trailer masquerading as the genuine original Hollywood operation. Because it is a petty jungle, cover your flank by hiring a faithful friend as a draftsman so that you are free to roam, to shop and to check on building, set erection, dressing and the general ennui.

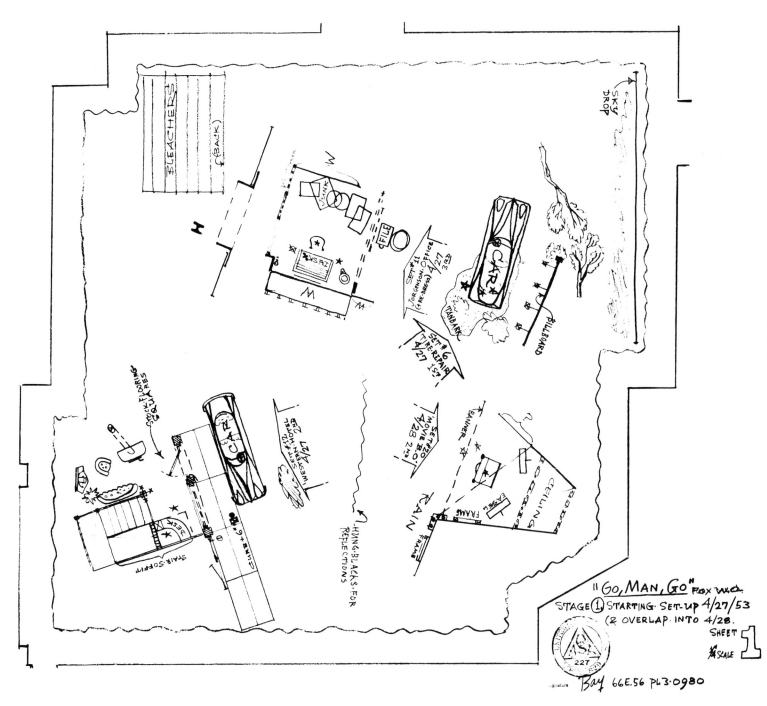

Howard Bay   "Go, Man, Go"   [film; spotting plan]   (1955)

159

Perhaps you wonder why I refer to politics ahead of loftier design-technical considerations. Politics looms large in the cinema and you must be warned or the loveliest sets will perish on the drawing board. Now about the artistic side: In an important sense film art direction is tougher than stage design; it is more apt to get out of hand. These days most of the footage is shot on location, so although you aid in finding locations, you are working backward from actuality, albeit a selective slice of actuality. For the art director the star word in the dictionary is *matching,* and it is hardly necessary to mention that total realism is the one and only prevailing mode. You can save your little box of water colors for Sundays in the park. That august art historian, Erwin Panofsky, wraps it up: "The processes of all the earlier representational arts conform, in a higher or lesser degree, to an idealistic conception of the world. These arts operate from top to bottom, so to speak, and not from bottom to top; they start from an idea to be projected into shapeless matter and not with the objects that constitute the physical world. The painter works on a blank wall or canvas which he organizes into a likeness of things and persons according to his idea (however much this idea may have been nourished by reality); he does not work with the things and persons themselves even if he works 'from the model' . . . . The same is true even of the stage designer with his empty and sorely limited section of space. It is the movies, and only the movies, that do justice to the materialistic interpreta- tion of the universe which, whether we like it or not, pervades contemporary civilization . . . To pre- stylize reality prior to tackling it amounts to dodging the problem. The problem is to manipulate and shoot nonstylized reality in such a way that the result has style. This is a proposition no less legitimate and no less difficult than any proposition in the older arts." The Vital Message: a personal way of making pictures is a limited and dated concept of dramatic design, and in film it is completely beside the point. It does not imply that one retreats to piling up neutral transplants from the real world, but rather that one discovers the precise forms and objects that are saturated with the emotional aura of a particular scene in a particular motion picture. Is is a tall order that takes you far from the drawing board, and it demands a tenacious hold on the ten thousand things that end up in front of the camera.

For the interiors that are still manufactured in the studios, solidity, finish and provision for a variety of camera angles are the nominal prerequisites. Solidity is no longer the exclusive concern of the woodworking shop, since both stock and custom textures and shapes are available in vacuum form sheets, with direct sculpting hacked out of styrofoam or modeled and cast. Wild walls allow the camera to poke its head in anywhere, and your quarter-inch-to-the-foot spotting of sets on the studio floor must leave operating room from all probable shooting directions. Celluloid templates of the common lenses' angles are an aid to these layouts. Many helpful hints could be laid end-to-end, but they are unnecessary because you will quickly become acclimated to the quaint terminology and the ceremonial practices of the studio inhabitants. What no one can fill you in on is an empathy for the eye of the camera, which sees differently than the eyes in your head. Short of purchasing your own camera and taking home movies the only passable warm-up is to get your hands on a pro view finder and lug it around and look at everything long and hard—much more valuable than reading Andrew Sarris. Another thing that your best friends won't tell you is that you must add non-essential extensions and byways and vistas to the stipulated acting area; these peripheral glimpses give reality to a locale. The long Establishing Shot where Hollywood displayed Production Values is dead and buried; if the director has a whim to pan into that throwaway corner you had better give it as much

Gene Callahan   "America, America"   [film; sketch by Harry Horner and Al Brenner]

love and attention and textural interest as the well-trod center of activity. Composition in films is not exactly what you learned in art school; in fact, the director's frame is the only composition-making instrument around. You have the interesting problem of making every component right and logical, singly and in any adjacent combination that the camera wishes to select. Just forget about centers of attention, dynamic axes, yardarm balances and other such two-dimensional thoughts.

Treatises on art direction often begin with continuity sketches or, as they say in ad agencies that mess around with TV commercials, story board visuals. It's a logical beginning because the underlying theory is so rational. Thumbnail sketches of the contents of each shot follow each other into the hundreds, right down to the fadeout. They have a twofold purpose: (1) to guide the director in his setups and (2) to illustrate what needs to be built. Aside from the fact that rarely is there time to complete these drawings, (1) the director does not wish to be guided in his setups but prefers to balance living actors with each other and with their environment, because they do not have the same weight and mixture as pencil lines on a piece of paper. Then there isn't any second point, is there? Perspective sketches crystallize director-designer discussions on mood but, of course, never replace models and plans.

Drafting differs from the theatrical variety only insofar as the layout step is often skipped and the shops build directly from the designer's elevations, because the breakup of units for handling is not critical. In limited studio space, setup and dressing time is critical, so all the ingredients should be poised on dollies eager to roll into the studio when the whistle blows.

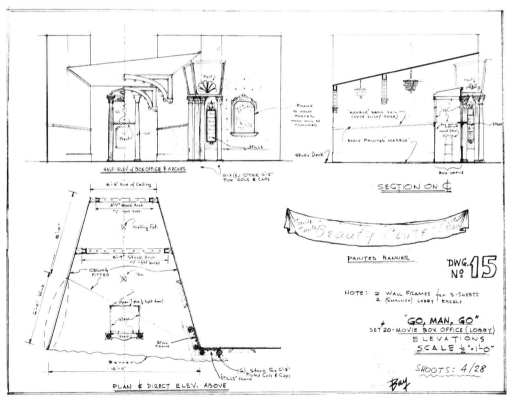

Howard Bay "Go, Man, Go"
[film; elevations] (1955)

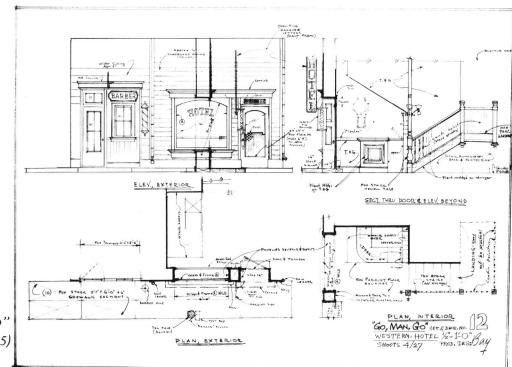

Howard Bay   *"Go, Man, Go"*
[*film; elevations*]   (1955)

Today television design is film design except for the once in a great while "specials" that sport smart displayish profiles against a cyc. Musicals and "imaginative" programs were on their way to finding a peculiarly television style when the industry picked up and went westward, and that was that. Employment is dispensed by the networks and the large films-for-TV companies; jobs rather than freelance contracts are the rule. The legendary cameraman Karl Fruend ground away at "I Love Lucy," and the fine art director Jack Martin Smith overlooks "Peyton Place," so don't look forward to unfettered creativity; a small swimming pool is in your future. Though the pay and the budgets are infinitesimal, Educational Television does try harder and it acts as a less soul-destroying initiation into the medium.

Industrial show is an umbrella term covering an uneasy blend of selling and entertainment that is usually aimed at sales conventions but may be offered to the public corralled at fairs and expositions.

When Detroit had millions in tax dollars to toss around and before those infernal VWs were multiplying like rabbits, the auto shows were a lucrative sideline for the indigent stage artiste. Those epics are well-nigh indescribable—Busby Berkeley only dealt on an elephantine scale in sentiment and strange, native sexual repressions. Picture the boys and girls of the chorus choreographing a wraparound windshield, skits purloined from the early editions of the Vanities angled toward marching out there and pushing those glorious hunks of chrome, a score patched out of twenty-seven bars cadged from bygone musical hits, cute animated cartoons of the fuel system, and climaxed with the company pilot, good old Wolfy, in a locker-room harangue about getting behind the wheel and clobbering the competition. These divertisements were served up at 9 a.m. for the salesmen who had not even begun to shake off last night's jollity.

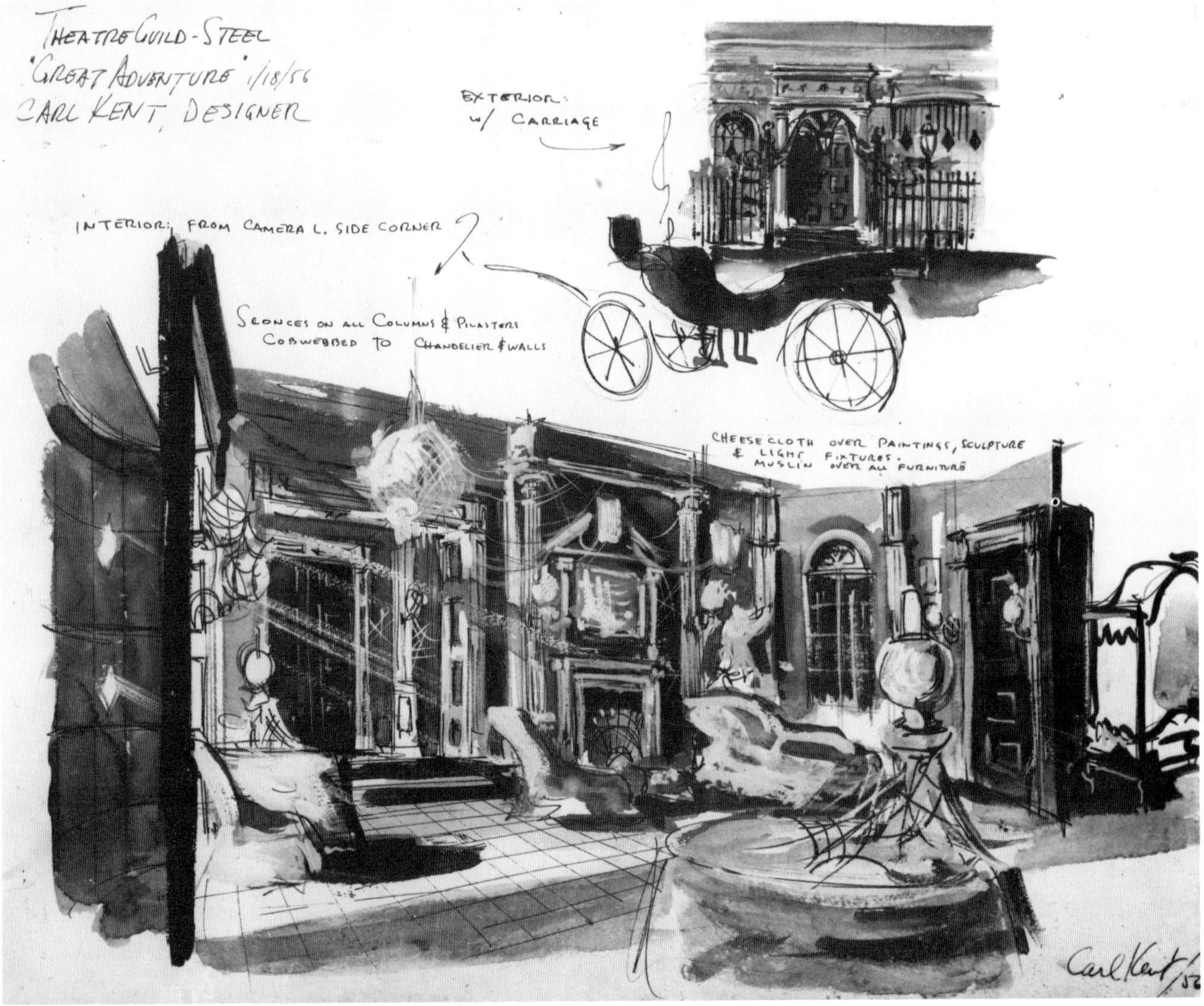
THEATRE GUILD - STEEL
'GREAT ADVENTURE' 1/18/56
CARL KENT, DESIGNER
EXTERIOR: w/ CARRIAGE
INTERIOR: FROM CAMERA L. SIDE CORNER
SCONCES ON ALL COLUMNS & PILASTERS
COBWEBBED TO CHANDELIER & WALLS
CHEESECLOTH OVER PAINTINGS, SCULPTURE
& LIGHT FIXTURES.
MUSLIN OVER ALL FURNITURE
Carl Kent/56

Carl Kent   Theatre Guild-U.S. Steel   [T.V.]   (1956)

These marvels might still be with us except for two events: the bottom fell out of the economy and the Montreal Expo swept in a whole new style of promotion. The dazzler was the Czech Pavilion, an avalanche of shifting, projecting and receding images that literally engulfed the beholder. The persuasive qualities of the still plus film plus actor total attack did not escape the hucksters. The Canadian Film Board added imaginative contributions. Multi-media's use to the drama is subject to debate, but its commercial exploitation is beyond question. Other hands can make films and figure out projection systems and chatter about engineering mysteries, but when it comes to wrapping it up in a dramatic parcel that attracts the citizenry, the scenic designer comes on with the grand vision. From Norman Bel Geddes's Futurama at the New York '39 Fair to Svoboda's Czech project and Sean Kenny's space affair at Montreal it has been the theatrical

Rouben Ter-Arutunian   "Taming of the Shrew"   [Hallmark T.V.]   (1956)

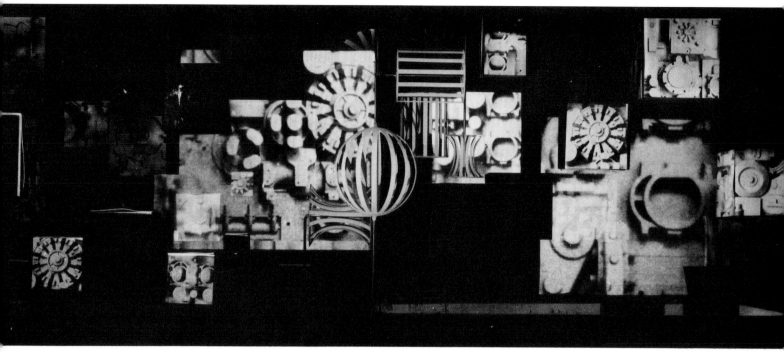

Josef Svoboda "Polyvision" (Montreal 1966)

designers who hurdle the nit picking and the cautious tiptoeing and make a big noise that heralds the future—the technological future, that is. Everyone else is hung up on pure form, a comfy womb that is as good as any other, I suppose. Do not get carried away and delude yourself into imagining that you are composing glorious dreams for Mankind; that is for the P.R. boys. This is salesmanship; it just isn't pure and simple any more. It is strobe, and lively kinetic doings, nothing staying put, exhilarating weightlessness—but you are there to push some facet of the status quo or the project wouldn't be underwritten, right? It is always nice to know precisely what you are doing, and you will probably do it better than the ostrich in the industrial design factory; prostitution has changed radically since Bette Davis in a flowered kimono. Your freelance, freewheeling attitude is more likely to come up with a new and different overall concept not revealed to the inmates of the advertising-architectural-commercial art complex. This brings up role playing, which you should perfect to get a peek at industrial design commissions. For a starter you might practice a young Frank Lloyd Wright (without the cane). Moody, rough hewn, contemptuous of shoddy commerce, equipped with carefully nonchalant sketchbooks resplendent with dream cities, inflatable mobile theatres and a fun palace on Mars. With sincere peasant dress, way-out friends spread around the rag trade and the arts, a hard agent who might arrange a squib in *New York Magazine*, you are on your way—to design a bath towel fashion show at the Sheraton-Hilton.

Whatever happened to Art In the Service of Industry? It is still around as one way to get bread, but the holy crusade and the tone poems have faded. It is high time the Bauhaus is finally laid to rest; Form

Follows Function has a lot to answer for. Buildings are not really machines—an object squeezed into a geometrical shape is not necessarily functional and what's more it may be inhuman and boring. Shiny cubes and cylinders might quite accidentally be something to sit on or in which to drop cigarette butts. We really don't need pristine purity in furnishings and appliances crowding into our personal islands of escape from the computers, now or in the foreseeable future.

The complex networks of technological services have replaced individual objects, and as a result industrial design has shifted to arbitrary packaging decor. This works to the advantage of the scenic designer as opposed to the Bauhaus disciple, who is all fouled up with outworn philosophical conditioning—abstractions tied to an earlier industrial civilization. The stage-trained artist studies the pertinent consumer desires and mocks up attractive containers that fulfill those desires. No homage to Good Design or what would Marcel Breuer say? Marketing Research and all sorts of testing surveys are the thing, but one bright-eyed, unprejudiced artist has been known to come through with the answer that has eluded statistical consensus. All the complicated psychological and social needs may be solved with a simple, intuitively arrived at gimmick.

Interior design divides up into the wholesale end, which is called contract work, and individual commissions. Contract work is the big money in suburban centers, motel chains, eatery chains, developments, banks, hospitals and company factories and offices, etc. It is catered by the big design firms that you may become affiliated with if you are so minded. Occasionally these firms go afield for a dramatic designer that

Josef Svoboda   "Polyvision"   (Montreal 1966)

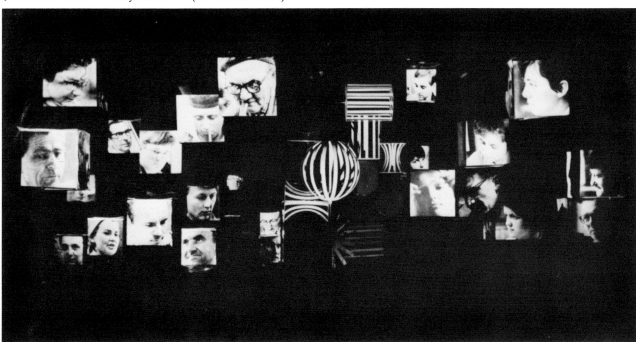

they think might add a little pizazz to a Vegas club or a palatial ballroom. I happened to be slaving on an extensive redo of the gambling rooms at the Hotel National when that Castro fellow marched in and decided on other uses for the facilities—no consideration for Private Enterprise. The jazzier stuff is more fun in a vulgar sort of way, unless you are fascinated with the cubic footage allotted to a bookkeeper or in plotting traffic patterns to the washrooms.

The private interior decorating scene is not in the pink of condition and not only because of the downbeat economy. You won't find discussions of the new depressant in the trade journals, but my survey points to the young and their disinterest in the whole subject of fancy, stable surroundings. And that is not the end of it; a chain reaction has set in that for the first time has jarred the oldsters. The parents are becoming a bit uncomfortable framed in blatantly opulent possessions. Drop dead affluence is curdling. Living For Young Homemakers is a dirty phrase, but more significantly, *House and Garden* is looking tatty. There will always be a *Town and Country*, but that hardly takes care of Grand Rapids, the Carolina factories, the fabric houses, the antique market, the myriad furnishing services, and your chances in the personal decor racket. Interior decoration has always been embroidery around the expensive edges of society, but now the expensive people are acting shy and retiring. Also, they have been getting around more and have noticed that royal folks don't live in museums assembled by French & Co.; their ottomans are shabby, tennis rackets are thrown in the corner, and generations of hounds have molested the Aubussons.

One worthy carryover from theatre into decoration is the whole idea of onstage and backstage, a separation that has always been a part of Oriental thinking. As we pass beyond the status exhibition of one's worldly goods, closets and other storage areas will hold the effects that are not in constant use. Peace and serenity flower in uncluttered space populated with only the necessary accessories for living—attractive things that the inhabitants like to sit on and handle and look at. An awful lot of product accumulation can be filed offstage awaiting its cue—or be consigned to the Goodwill Industries.

Although it will give no immediate warmth, I will whisper that when you make any sort of Name in the theatre you will automatically attract decorating nibbles from breathless ladies who want Something Different and Exciting. For conversational purpose you absolutely cannot top, "Oh yes, I was advised by . . . you know, who just did those stunning sets for . . . " Advised, hah! Oh, you need a refill, you look positively glum I caught you muttering in your beard . . . why don't you grow a beard, it would be cute, my husband is so stuffy about beards . . . the children . . . .

Even if you have an urge to beautify our Land with a less remunerative brand of design that has nothing to do with Prestige and Taste, you still should join the National Society of Interior Designers. They will give you a card entitling you to professional trade discounts which are considerable. I almost said "brand of rational design," but I couldn't go that far, for there is something abnormal about filling up other people's homes, about being a specialist in strangers' living rooms. As a calling it will ultimately wither away. It is not an extension of dramatic design; it is pointed in the opposite direction. The mission of dramatic design is to reveal character, to uncover truths—Need I go on? It is refreshing that the Beatles have supplanted Louis XIV as models, the images we project on our domiciles, but it is still role playing. It is harmless enough, and rather poignant. I merely point out that one should know what one is doing, which in the case of home decoration is to aid the client in building a nest in the shape of the imaginary personality he wishes

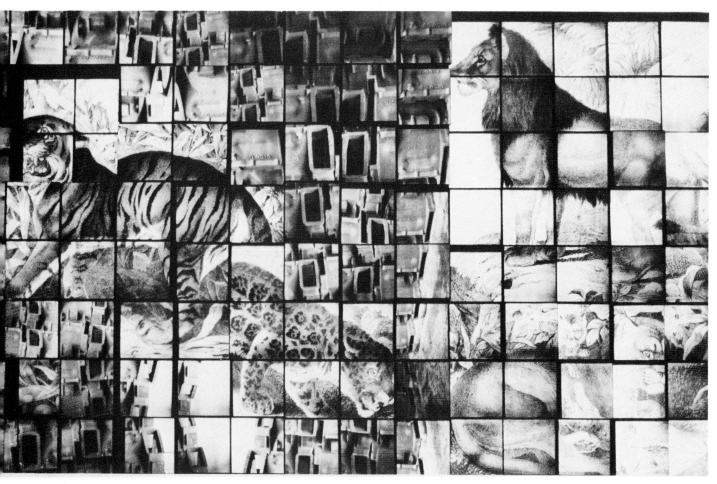

Josef Svoboda "*Diapolyecran*" *(Montreal 1966)*

to exhibit. It has nothing to do with your own precious artistic preferences, and here we bump into a sticky one. The *business* of interior decoration is exhibitionism on wheels: create a Style, your own personal trademark, and stamp it loud and clear on every portion of every job if you want to Get Talked About. Glancing around the apartments gussied up by Noted Decorators you are affected with the queasy sensation that the inhabitants don't even possess imaginary personalities. It all started with sprightly dialogue about bringing out the Real You, but in the end, peas in a pod. No wonder the young instinctively gravitate toward the artist's studio, which is just a cleaned up, whitewashed place containing just what is needed for work and play. Perhaps some pleasant things picked up here and there; but when it explodes into a whole kooky deal you know someone is straining for a spread on the fashion page of the *Times* and we might as well be back with Elsie de Wolfe.

Among other possible lines of expansion: Abe Feder, a theatrical colleague, in his own spectacular manner has led the way in commercial lighting, which is duck soup to the stage illuminator. Otherwise . . . the display industry is a decidedly underpaid affair, and I have never figured out what the word "communications" means.

This once-over-lightly list of the tangents open to the scenic designer is put down merely to convey an aroma of the realistic possibilities. Your temperament and job opportunities will pick up from here.

VIII.
Theatrical Space

"A theatre is a creative environment for hundreds of craftsmen, who from time to time, will call this surrounding their own place of work. Architecture must reflect all the experiences, past, present and future of these craftsmen, the actors, directors, composers, designers and technicians. Architecture must comprehend the total objective and subjective experience of these artists.

"It would seem then that one with a vast theatre knowledge and experience himself would best be equipped to put a theatre building together. It is he who would be most able to render the best judgments of his consulting specialists for the best possible theatre for all concerned." Ralph Alswang.

The above statement by an active designer and theatre consultant is a truth that seems self-evident. But theatre architecture, to judge from the examples springing up all over our landscape, takes off from a totally opposite premise, namely, that a theatre building should advertise the aesthetic stance of the architect-creator. It is conceivable that certain structures should reflect the latest in the formal modeling of space, but envelopes for dramatic activity are not it. Honestly, theatres are buildings where actors and audiences meet, nothing else. No positive statement in outsized sculpture can contain the unpredictable, mercurial, expanding and contracting substance that is living theatre. It is not surprising that many of the notorious fiascoes have been erected by our most esteemed architectural figures; the stronger the impact of the edifice the tighter the bonds constricting the freedom of the dramatic fare within. It is discouraging that builders of buildings for the drama do not grasp a basic fact: The Actor Is the Space Modulator, The Articulator of Volume, rather than the provider of bricks and mortar that keep out the elements. Most of the brand-new Cultural Centers, of course, are beyond the pale because they are merely status monuments, with no thought given to probable tenants. As Sean Kenny said, "The trouble is reinforced concrete foundations—let's find out first in what direction our theatre is heading." Houses that accommodate opera, ballet, musicals and other touring companies lay down cut-and-dried demands: a sufficient number of seats to satisfy economic demands, liberal space for scenery storage and scene shifting, a standard grid system, decent sight lines, easy loading access, dressing rooms, rehearsal rooms, a trapped stage, a large orchestra pit, audience facilities, perhaps a shop, etc. See "Theatre Check List" prepared by the American Theatre Planning Board, Wesleyan Press. (Just don't swallow the Beaumont, the Loeb or the UCLA plans as anything worth emulating.) Disaster strikes when a progressive architect brushes aside any of these needs because they appear old hat and boring and why can't we do something different and contemporary. He rules out the booking of certain attractions that take care of the overhead. He would do less damage if he were to confine himself to a stunning façade and Barcelona chairs in the lounges. Apart from differences in decorative tastes there is very little one can say about proscenium auditoriums that must be congenial hosts for varied imported fare.

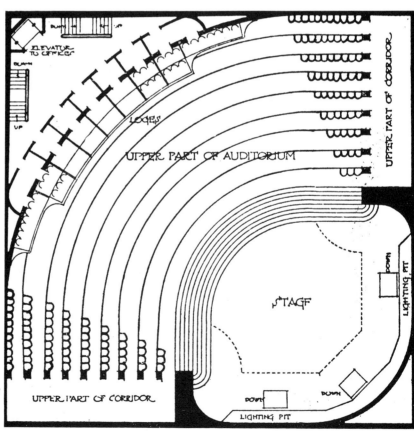

Norman Bel Geddes   Theatre Number Six 1921

All Purpose Theatre is rapidly becoming the nastiest phrase in the English language. Even architects and engineers are giving up the futile struggle to cram grand opera and closet drama into the same habitat. Sliding panels and hydraulic elevators cannot make a laboratory for artificial insemination feel cozy. What the slide-rule boys have difficulty grasping is the atmosphere of theatre, and a mighty elusive quality it is, too. It is a brew of warmth, just the right scale, the expectation of something special and, if lucky, the Ghosts of Past Glories. The last ingredient may be created without pomposity with crystal and other mystery-laden elements. It is not germaine that Mies, Gropius and Corbusier would not sanction such baubles; P. T. Barnum and Will Shakespeare would—and don't be so sure that Brecht wouldn't enjoy a little elegance out front. At all costs one must avoid antiseptic solemnity and the oppressive vulgarity of the State Theatre, the Kennedy Center, and the Met Opera, for example.

In the matrix of audience-facing-acting-area-in-a-frontal-viewing-relationship the only revisions that are here to stay are the expansion of apron into thrust stage and its corollary, the slurring of the proscenium arch, minimizing the frame and merely opening up on backstage. Walling up the rear of the thrust stage with a permanent structure of levels, stairs and entrances has proved obtrusive and inflexible for a wide repertory; there are oodles of plays that can't abide choreographed pages moving furniture. Example: I directed a college production of John Arden's *The Workhouse Donkey,* and Arden said he preferred it to

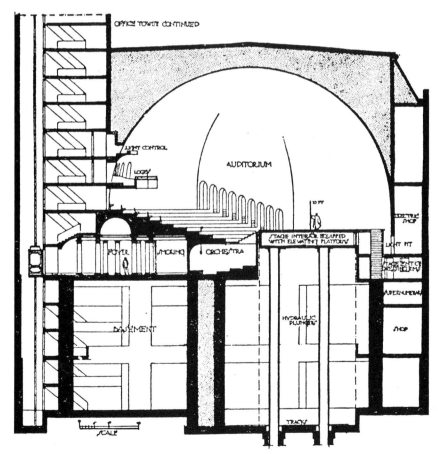

Norman Bel Geddes   Theatre Number Six 1921

Hellerau Theatre (1912)

the Chichester British National Theatre presentation. Unable to credit the superiority solely to my student cast and my sterling staging, I questioned Arden on the Chichester mounting. Forced by their permanent setting and naked thrust to integrate visibly the multiple changes of furniture and properties, music was composed to accompany the set and strike movement pattern, thus adding nigh unto fifteen minutes to a very long show. *Donkey* resists cutting because its many plots and subplots make quite a tangle and interlarded are musical turns that must stay because they are half the fun. At Brandeis we devised a wagon arc (with identical formal backgrounds on the two segments) and reduced all changes to twelve seconds. Our *Donkey* tumbled along at a brisk clop.

   Plans and even models are unsatisfactory skeletons of actual, finished, functioning theatre structure—the gestalt of mood, scale, audience-actor contact that makes the difference between dramatic excitement and just dead enclosed space that may reproduce well in *Architectural Forum.* Actors and other stage workers seldom cover theatre buildings for architectural publications.

   Peter Brook in *The Empty Space,* the most sensible look at today's theatre available at your bookstore, goes beyond our obvious point that unlike a hospital it doesn't do to analyze the requirements of a theatre, feed them into the computer, and take a compass and a ruler and add up the findings. He maintains that the sacred, remote and hence dead theatre must be broken up by the rough, bawdy, perhaps disordered atmosphere of a truly intimate, lively, popular theatre housing. A milder variation of this theme is Hugh Hardy's argument for structures that allow for peripheral vision, things going on all over the place, random focus, rather than Architecture that is expensive and forever. It is sad and significant that Norman Bel Geddes's unrealized Theatre Number Six dreamed up in 1921 is a more imaginative solution for the fixed element theatre format than anything rising around us today. Now we would shrink Number Six a bit to lose the cathedral air, but otherwise it bespeaks a neutrality that could contain a wide spectrum of events. It neatly jumps over the question of a little or a great deal of scenery as there is no frame to fill; for frontal seating this is unique. Also, you can project at will anywhere or everywhere on the dome that encloses both audience and players. Beat that with the latest engineering shenanigans—even when they get the bugs out.

In the historical forebears line, Dalcroze's Hellerau theatre, 1912, masterminded by Adolphe Appia, is closer to our present tastes. It was merely a rectangular hall with no break between auditorium and stage and with translucent walls that could be colored at will.

An analysis of the topsy-like growth of the conventional playhouses by the Bortnovskis and Ciulei translated from the Roumanian is reprinted in *Theatre Design and Technology* (Number 12, May 1968). However, the clever solution is too clever, diffused and mechanical. Incidentally, the most frightening mechanical monster is the cylinder-revolve imbedded in the Vienna Burgtheatre. By contrast one should peruse the clean, homespun, economy-size, pictorial open stages by James Hull Miller sprinkled throughout the midwest. Just drop a postcard to Hub Electric, Chicago, and receive your illustrated booklet. Ingenious, inexpensive and varied auditoriums; the disturbing reservation is that in many structures one is struck with projected scenery from now to eternity.

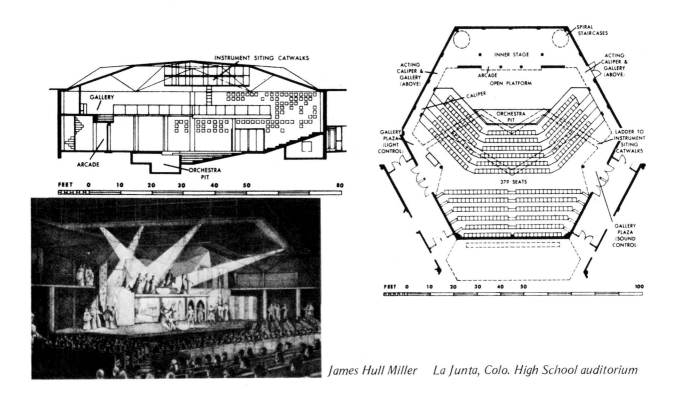

James Hull Miller   La Junta, Colo. High School auditorium

Page references for illustrations

172
173

175

A. L. Ledesma   "Dr. Faustus" (Mexico City 1966)

Original Arena Stage
(Washington, D.C., 1961)
Harry Weese, architect

But the news bulletin is that we are wandering away from the block of customers facing the stage head-on. Not that opera, ballet and fat musicals won't be there when we wake up tomorrow morning, but that Forward-Looking serious drama is impatiently scratching around for new environments and different audience-actor blends. Firehouses, railway roundhouses, garages and lofts are being dusted off, and ex-houses of worship are being picked up at bargain prices. It would be an error to label this drive rambling financial expediency or quaint torchbearing perversity or a Back to the Catacombs. It is just the beginning. It is a determined flight from the affluent, prestige connotations congealed in the established playhouse. It is a drive to start anew, far away from the weight of historical precedents. To quote Sean Kenny once again, it is a yearning for "a clean white-canvas place." No thought is given to Architectural Standards—flexible seating in an "experimental" theatre in a Lincoln Center doesn't really interest the New Theatre mob at all. It matters not a whit to them if the style of a special new building devoted to the Drama is conservative, radical, neo-romantic or brut; it is filed under Their Imperial Monuments. So pushing aside the stupendous and irrelevant projects for automated temples of the performing arts, what do the young Thespians have in mind in the line of physical surroundings? Well, not much at the moment, with the wholesale demolition of the past at the top of the agenda. When the crash diet of actors plus friends on hard benches plus a few old spotlights doesn't seem to win audiences—and the turning point into reality and on the road toward worthy theatre is the cold recognition of the need to uncover ways and means of winning audiences —then the designer will come forward. Although theatre can flourish in the damnedest places under the most exasperating handicaps, it is valuable to examine the predictable needs of the New Theatre and offer one possible answer in project form. A graduate design class at Brandeis worked out a scheme predicated on

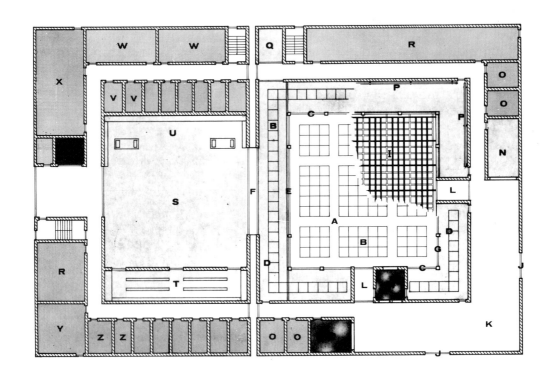

A Theatre Space: 60'x60'x18'	N Coat Rooms
B Trapped Floor: 4'x4'	o Rest Rooms
c Wing Doors: 18' high	P Light Instrument Storage
D Wings: 12' deep	Q Freight Elevator
E Sliding Doors: 36' wide	R Management
F Sliding Walls: 36' wide	s Shop
G Wing Doors: 8' high	T Tool Room
H Booth: 60' long	U Paint Area & Frame
I Interchangable Grid	v Dressing Rooms
J Main Entrances	w Chorus
K Lobby	
L Anterooms	
M Box Office	

x Greenroom
y Conference Room
z Live Storage
1 Technical Office
2 Design & Work Areas
3 Rehearsal Room
4 Permanent Grid
5 Dead Storage
6 Trap Room
7 Hydraulic Elevator

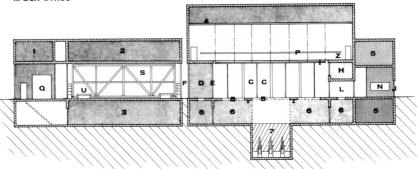

Victor Becker   Flexible theatre project (Brandeis University, 1971)

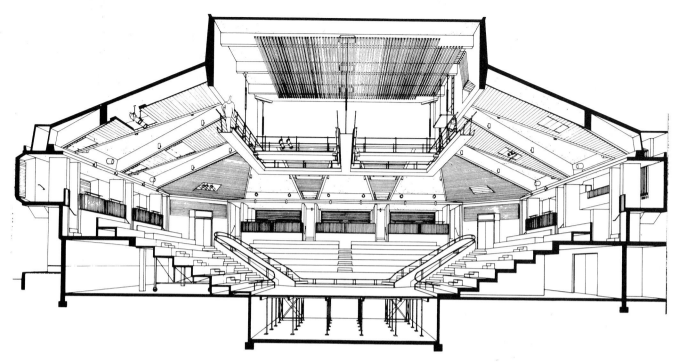

Original Arena Stage [cross section] (Washington, D.C., 1961)

the assumption that New Theatre will be a self-propelled, tight production group for quite a spell; flexible intimacy is therefore the keynote. The booking-in of conventional attractions is left to the conventional houses. In many respects it parallels the University of Texas 350-seat experimental housing, but with one difference. We attempted to minimize the mechanics required and to concentrate on a warm neutral space. Let Me Make This Perfectly Clear: this was a classroom exercise, a smallish examination of elastic geography and an unobtrusive skin for innovative drama; it escapes the contradictions of the grandiose structures only in *degree* of building and maintenance costs. The revamping of existing buildings is apt to be more sensible.

I could apologize for not reproducing fascinating plans and sections and photos of theatres springing up around the globe, but I won't apologize because (1) prints and photos do not communicate the atmosphere and rightness or wrongness of a theatre, and (2) it may well be that the concrete and electronic wonders have nothing to do with the theatre even a decade hence. For a panorama of advanced international theatre building wizardry, examine *The Modern Theatre* by Hannelore Schubert.

This brusque chapter must be filled out by reading Mielziner's *The Shapes of Our Theatre*. His lucid, diagrammatic coverage of all the formal historical configurations of audience-player combinations has arrived not a moment too soon. It just may prevent erecting a few more monstrosities. One wishes that Mielziner had not been so delicate about architects' responsibility for the many Houses of Horror, but then it would be bad business to endanger consulting commissions from architectural firms, wouldn't it?

Kreeger Arena Stage   (Washington, D.C., 1971)   Harry Weese, architect

I rather doubt that there will be many rational theatre buildings as long as the architect is in the driver's seat. The only sane structures have been dictated by performing companies, such as the Washington Arena, the Houston Alley and the Cincinnati Playhouse in the Park. Here the architects were builders who knew their place, to wit: to execute the needs of the tenants—precise needs collected over years of experience. The artistic ego of the architect is not the lead villain in the piece, although it breeds harmful side effects, such as battalions of consultants who are not independent authorities but specialized stooges. The mealy core is the bejeweled lump of culture vultures who are happy and proud of gigantic, drop-dead lobbies, bronze plaques and gala openings but offer nary a penny for maintenance or what goes on behind the gold curtain. Ere the first snow blanketed the Henry Moore in the promenade an ulcerous manager was out booking a disguised skin flick festival to defray the janitor's salary. Really, what are those drama students doing down there in that messy storefront—in a disreputable part of town, too. Where do they find a place to park the Porsche?

A witty and perceptive digging into the root causes of the deplorable building saddling the spoken drama has been written by Donald C. Mullin, *The Development of the Playhouse.* He observes, "Seldom has the theatre structure been allowed to take its own necessary form and shape. Almost always it has been corseted into a form more consistent with current ideas about what is real and true, or what is respectable

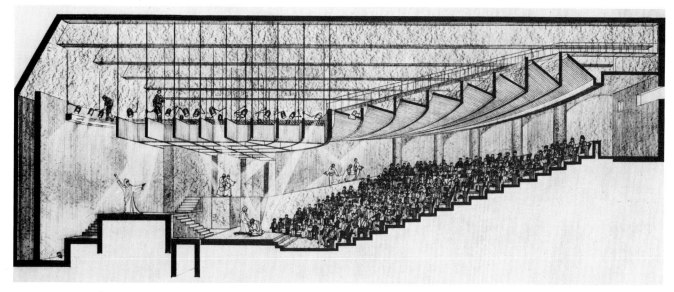

Alley Theatre   (Houston, 1970)   Ulrich Franzan and Associates, architects

and therefore worth preserving. A continuous thread that runs through theatre architectural theories (as well as through other forms of theatrical expression) is the not-quite-repressed suspicion that drama actually died 2500 years ago, and all we have been doing since is merely mummery and dumbshow. Buildings reflecting permanent and responsible attitudes, then, have been the goal of almost every theatre architect from Palladio onward. We have been exposed to a long series of apologies for theatre, a series that has not stopped to this day."

Mr. Mullin carries on with appropriate sarcasm for the archeological copybook mausoleums in the classical mold, the Age of Reason with geometry as the Final Solution, the absurd end of the Theatre as Classroom in the Mass Pageants for the populace, electro-mechanical legerdemain as its own argument for

Cincinnati Playhouse in the Park   (1969)
Hardy Holzman Pfeiffer Associates, architects

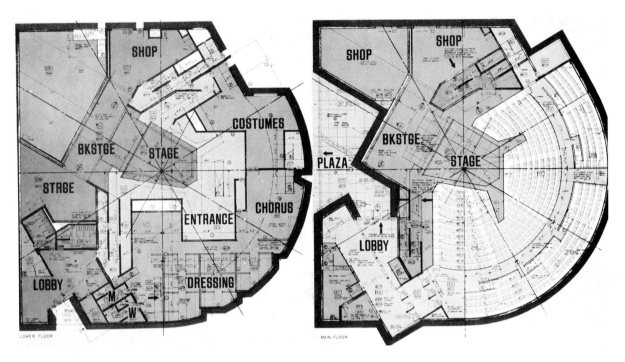

Cincinnati Playhouse in the Park   (1969) Hardy Holzman Pfeiffer Associates, architects

existence—the fascinating show the audience never sees, architectural arrogance in the Theatre As Sculpture, the fragmentation of audiences in Temples of Alienation, etc., etc.

I shall add to Mullin's wry list one more cause of the concrete chaos: the Emperor's New Clothes bit is such a popular craze because everyone is selling something, usually himself—from foundations and donors through architects, consultants, builders, equipment firms, trade periodicals, to the civic leaders and the institutions of learning who lust after a larger and fancier showcase than their next door neighbor's. I am plagued with the recurrent dream of Bobby Clark crashing through a Philip Johnson glass portal, crawling over a Tony Smith seesaw vainly seeking a place to deposit his chewing gum, methodically hanging out the wash on the Lippold chandelier, sneaking into the control booth and with maniacal concentration punching buttons on the super-console causing the audience to be dumped into the cellar and the orchestra to be shunted into the refreshment area. I invariably awake when the light pipes descend, slicing and dicing the actors spinning around on the berserk revolving stage.

IX.
Trappings for the New Stagecraft

It is regrettable that we cannot briskly rustle up an impressive inventory of helpful hints for the student designer who will sally forth to engage the New Theatre. Time must be consumed merely conjecturing on the nature of the creature.

Although the label New Theatre is tossed around a lot, there is precious little New Theatre playing tonight. All the rumpus about taking clothes off or keeping them on, will multi-media replace round actors, have the Becks the inalienable right to spit in your eye (let's stick to the Liberal rules, OK fellas?), should characters run up and down the aisles, etc., etc., is obviously not it. We do know that the whole literary-dramatic theatre is manipulated by the Amusement Industry—our own little Establishment. To bandy about the label Establishment may seem capricious at first blush. Can this grab bag of double-breasted flesh merchants, midget promoters and occasional tourists from solid commerce add up to an Organization as we picture a Seat of Power? An adequate answer with documentation would require a sturdy volume, but the answer is yes. The Arts are not set in motion by directives sent down from the thirty-third floor of a Rockefeller Center, but underneath all the cultural frosting is either an unstated or an unconscious allegiance to the status quo. Once in a while the drama may appear uppity and daring because it is such a fringe activity that self-indulgent motives toss surplus tax and inheritance monies to modish evenings of anarchism and defeatism. The artists of the theatre can be relied on not to Stray Beyond the Pale because It Would Not Occur To Them—Doesn't Everyone Appreciate Shakespeare? Little Eva En Route To Heaven had

Josef Szajna   "Smierć na Gruszy"
(Warsaw, 1968)

Josef Szajna   "November Dictum"
(Warsaw, 1969)

heavier thoughts on the Big Picture than do the voting majority of the Dramatists' Guild. What G. Moses calls "the un-agitational propaganda theatre" not only pilfers the best talent but appropriates the idea and surface styles of the artistic Left, so Far-Out dressing is no criterion: *Hair, Oh, Calcutta, Company—Follies, J. C. Superstar*, are nice retrogressive affairs at heart. Tom O'Horgan always folds up the flag neatly. Nor are the Showcases for New Dramatists New Theatre; such outfits carrying out their worthy task on the margins of commercial theatre are necessarily temporary, manic-depressive combines—extensions of traditional craft and prevailing modes, as subservient to the one-show economy as the League of New York Theatre. If the title New Theatre is to retain any significance, it should be restricted to a dedicated, disciplined, long-term performance group united by a vision and led by an inspired director. Well, that sort of bypasses the current crop of companies in the U.S.A. This hole may be plugged up, mainly due to the precepts and example of a few Poles—if they will only let up on pompous seminars around here. The awesome fanaticism of Jerzy Grotowski's Polish Lab Theatre is not likely to be duplicated in America because of our impatience with rigorous training, our pampering of the actor's ego; but the inspirational drive of his band must plant seeds even in our permissive and woozy theatrical climate. We don't possess the imagination to envisage American translations free of the ghosts of the Polish medieval church and slanted toward our crush on clowns and slapstick. While Grotowski's pronouncements, rather sloppily collected in *Towards a Poor Theatre*, are must reading for serious type theatre laborers, his co-philosopher, Ludwik Flaszen's "After the Avant Garde" (from the Polish Theatre Magazine) is worth reprinting in full:

"We are to speak of the situation in contemporary theatre. The task is a very difficult one simply because the term 'situation' implies a particular, determined state, while most characteristic for today's theatre is the state of 'indetermination'. The statistics of theatrical life will not help us much; it is obvious that its atmosphere is rather diluted.

"The most famous comtemporary playwrights are known as 'the avant-garde of the 50s and 60s'. The formula contains a certain distance characteristic for historical terminology. These were the authors who shook the traditional image of the theatre, who showed the possibility of a new sensitivity, who have ruined the language; what was left was only silence and immobility. In this sense the work of Beckett is truly great in its daring to go to the most extreme consequences. His ideal would be a dark and empty stage from which not a sound would reach the audience. But the wave of destruction dating from the 50s and 60s has passed. May these famous authors live a long and happy life and provide us with surprises; most probably, even certainly, their work is finished. The most important question now, I believe, is what the future developments will be.

"In all truth we must say that the above authors leave behind not so much a new theatre, as literary works written for the stage. They leave us theatrical scores, but not a new genre of acting. They do not propose a new function for the theatre, but a revolt against the old function of which the revolt was part. Is the change, now that the first strong impression is gone, that great? I am afraid that the fate of every theatrical avant-garde might be repeated; since the time of Craig every one of them left behind written evidence—the utopia of various possibilities. And, from time to time, ephemeral practical attempts. As long as Beckett's plays are produced we shall deal with a new form of the theatre, though grafted on the old one; when we have enough of Beckett, the good old theatrical junk will be back.

"So what? What do we propose after the avant-garde? When we started our work in 1959 in a small Silesian town in the western part of Poland, we did not consciously ask this question. In reality, though, we took over the inheritance of these avant-garde writers. When Grotowski produced the first plays in his Laboratory Theatre, he did not intend to outdo Beckett. We did not even produce the avant-garde plays which were at the time so fashionable in Poland. We have produced, and are still doing it, Polish and international masterpieces which in our culture have a generalizing function similar to that of myths. We felt that it was extremely difficult to do anything new in the theatre since the avant-garde had reached the end of its possibilities.

Mrkvicka, Teige & Zelenka "Prsy Tiresiovy" (Prague, 1926)

"And, after all, this dramaturgy has changed very little on the Polish stage; the stage designs moved in the direction of the avant-garde, but the actors remained faithful to the old cliches with which they mixed a bit of clowning and a cold, mechanic diction considered in some circles to be the style of contemporary acting. The avant-garde provided a consistent model for the drama. It was necessary, though, to start thinking of that in the theatre which is not the word, to think about the theatre.

"As far as the situation of the theatre in the contemporary world is concerned, our hypothesis is pessimistic. The role of the theatre is narrowing and its prestige is lowering. The attention of the audience is directed toward other kinds of entertainment, better adapted to the speed of contemporary life. It is not merely a matter of competition. In this changing world, in which all traditional communities, their values and rites, are breaking down, the place of theatre in social life is rather vague. What is the theatre? A temple? A stadium? The agora? A marketplace? A tribune? A courtly ceremonial? A carnival custom? To say the truth, today it can be all of these things thanks to stylization which is a recognized sign of semi-commitment. And what about commitment that is complete and serious, that goes beyond aesthetic trifle and entertainment? The theatre is still the favorite subject for lonely maniacs. And the realization of the situation of a lonely maniac can provoke pathetic authenticity. The time of great holiday ceremonials, miracle plays and meetings, of carnivals and Dionysian festivals is gone; the only thing left for the theatre is noble solitude. If we should treat it seriously, as a particular form of life, what is the theatre today? It is a hermitage where a dying art is practiced. Paradoxically, that is where it realizes its similarity with Job deprived of his riches and dignity, and the possibility of revival: *Credo quia absurdum.*

"Ionesco described one of his plays as 'a tragedy of language.' The formula has a generalizing value for the avant-garde works of the 50s. Because of its mechanical nature, language cannot express the truth. The word is an imposter and creates an agglomeration of automatic absurds, as in Ionesco; a vicious circle of pleonasms, as in Beckett; and an endless dialectic of appearances and reality, as in Genet. The language, the text—this element of discursive clarity, is reaching the end of its possibilities. The avant-garde has proved it in the theatre by means of this same language and text. A fundamental reflection on the theatre forces us to go further. To create a theatre we must go beyond literature, because theatre starts where the word is not sufficient. Artaud knew, and realized it in his dreams, that the language of the theatre cannot be the language of words, that it must be its own language fused with its very nature. He realized it in dreams only—this is where those who quote and apply his words are wrong; they go no further than theatrical rhetoric. Artaud is a saint. Let us pray to him and hope that he does not descend from the altar.

"The same thought which sees in the theatre's solitude its chance for future development tells us to go beyond the discursive word, tells us to dismiss everything that is not necessary for the theatrical phenomenon, to leave only that without which it cannot exist. It can do without stage sets, without pasted-on noses, without make-up, the play of lights, music, without any technical effects. But it cannot exist without the actor, without the live contact between people, the kind of contact that arises between the actor, his partner, and the audience. The proper subject-matter of the theatre, its particular score unattainable for other arts, is—as Grotowski puts it—the score of human impulses and reactions, the psychic process exposed via bodily and vocal reactions of the human organism. This is the theatre's essential subject-matter.

"Attempting to go beyond the rhetorical and illusional theatre, today's directors, those who consider themselves modern, try to achieve their goal by multiplying mechanic, visual effects or by realizing the synthesis of arts. This form of the theatre endlessly repeats its matter, its means and effects, and is called the total theatre. Lost in external visual effects, dissolute in the din of concrete music, it loses that which is the modest but pure essence of the theatre. Antithetic to this rich theatre is the poor theatre realized by Grotowski; the world of this theatre is built of the actor's impulses and reactions.

"Let us not multiply effects, but rather eliminate them. If today's theatre is like Job deprived of his heritage, it should at least have the awareness of its fate. Let it shed all appearances and concentrate on that in which it is unique. Let it make a force out of its poverty.

Yannis Kokkos   "La Guerre de Troie"
(Paris, 1971)

Howard Bay   "one third of a nation"   (Poughkeepsie, 1937)

"The avant-garde of the 50s and 60s has proved that the traditional tragic quality can no longer be sustained in the theatre. The tragic sense can exist only when values have a transcendental guarantee, when they are considered to be a kind of substance. When gods die, the grotesque, the painful grimace of the clown facing the empty sky takes the place of tragedy. The traditional tragic sense has become today a dry, lofty rhetoric or a trivial, tearful melodrama. The question is how to achieve in the theatre a tragic quality which would not become merely a stiff and picturesque pose, which would go beyond harlequinade. How can the old feelings of pity and terror, long lost in our emotional memory, be reawakened? The practical answer can be reached in going beyond the elementary final values. In the last resort, the whole of the human organism belongs here. When there is nothing else left, the body, the living organism which is the material guarantee of human independence, of our distinctness in relation to the rest of the world, becomes the asylum of human dignity. In effect of a paradoxical convolution the actor reaches pathos when he reveals his intimate, inner feelings embodied in the material reactions of the organism, when his soul seems to become pure physiology, when he presents himself to the public unarmed and naked, and offers his weakness to the cruelty of his partners and the audience. Values are reborn on a higher plane when the audience undergoes a shock. The totally uncovered misery of the human condition, sincere beyond what is considered as

188

good manners and good taste, reaching a peak and becoming a transgression, produces a purification of an archaic form. An example of this understanding of the tragic quality is 'The Constant Prince' in Grotowski's staging.

"At a time when a rapid evolution of our civilization mixes the happiness of conquering with the suffering of being uprooted, and when the traditional disciplines and arts are losing their vital function, we are turning back to the theatre, to its archaic sources. The goal of Grotowski's productions is to reawaken the utopia of elementary emotions produced by a common rite, by ecstatic exaltation in which the community dreamed about its own essence, placed itself in total reality, a reality which was not broken into various spheres, where Beauty did not differ from Truth, or feeling from intellect, body from soul, happiness from suffering; where man seemed to feel a union with the whole of Being. Experience has led us to the theatre of miracle plays. How can a theatre of miracle plays be created at a time when rites are dying out and dispersing, when the dispersed rites have no universal value? How can one create a secular miracle play, a contradiction in terms? A miracle play which would not be a mere stylization of the old plays, a purely aesthetic performance? It can be achieved through a profanation of myths and rites, through blasphemy. This kind of transgression brings back their basic background and plunges us into terror. But this happens on the human plane, outside the cult. The essence of the rite is its non-temporal character; all of its action is renewed each time in its obvious and real presence. The rite does not present past history but that which happens all the time, *hic et nunc*. What does this mean for the theatre? The time of theatrical action is the same as

Howard Bay   "Dog Beneath the Skin"   (1938)

Howard Bay *"Life and Death of an American"* *(New York, 1939)*

the time of the production. The production is not an illusionary copy of reality, neither is it an imitation or a set of conventions accepted as a kind of conscious play. The production is a literal, obvious fact. It does not exist outside of its own matter. The actor does not act, imitate, or pretend. He is himself in a public act of confession. His inner processes are his own and not the work of a clever artist. In this theatre the aim is not the literal fact—no one bleeds or dies—but rather the literal spiritual act to which Grotowski's method leads the actor. Our work is an attempt to restore the archaic values of the theatre. We are not modern; on the contrary, we are quite traditional. It could even be said that we are rather the rear guard than the avant-garde. It happens that most surprising are those things which have already taken place in the past. Their novelty is the more impressive the greater the time lapse which separates us from them."

If to our rich tastes the Grotowski-Flaszen road is too much like taking the vows, and our chaotic entertainment structure rules out holding a company together for a sufficient time span to build a cohesive style, let us turn to another Pole, artist-director-designer Jozef Szajna (from an interview in the Polish 184 Theatre Magazine). The loosely-knit fragments not only conjure up the shape of a Total-Open Theatre but project the expanding function of the designer in the creation of one brand of vanguard theatre.

"Penetration of life is based essentially on the questioning of known truths and acting against the fetishism of objects. The growing discrepancies between man and the surrounding world seem to be averting the time of affirmation. Making use of the human mind for barbaric goals forces us to rescue what is left of human dignity. The creative act denies the nothingness of man. The moment of creation as the most personal act of choice, the moment when the object created in the atmosphere of the artist's feelings is freed and set in the sphere of meaning, is a moment of action, a manifestation of an extreme involvement in life. It is an attitude which contradicts passivity. . . .

"The 'open theatre,' related to contemporary thought, and not concerned with superficial aesthetics, the theatre of innovation, the total theatre in which the value scheme of the subject—i.e., the personalities of its creators—permeates the drama, such theatre is capable of complete conveyance ('visualization') through a complex method of integration of elements. Directing and the arts complement each other and create an unbroken whole. The construction of the performance consists of imagined stage happenings, of fictitious and imagined situations. The proposed 'playgame' may be, in real life, hardly probable. The whole thing takes place in a rather undefined time, the passing of which becomes unimportant. It is a montage of action in which a number of facts, seemingly unrelated, become united into the anecdote of 'sensation.' The mechanics is in the representation and the movement of events, which lay open the interdependence of characters and things, of objects and ideas. The play of opposites and discords is the arsenal, and at the same time the peculiar 'harmony' of these productions. Stage sets disappear, and what we see is the representation of images composed and directed with the use of objects which participate in the action and even interfere in it. This kind of stage setting loses the characteristics of mere decor, of an architectural fragment, and becomes the matter of the theatrical process. It becomes independent of the author's stage directions, and gains autonomous value, becomes 'the space of expression.' It does not describe the place and time of action, but uses concrete, often ready objects which participate in the theatrical action. The action takes place in empty spaces, or in open, deserted spaces. . . .

"Any object taken out of its natural surroundings can become a 'decor sign' or a part of the adapted space. The actors' use of objects which are partners, and which are quite different from the props of the theatre of manners, is subdued to the intellectual and formal unity of the production—manifestation. The objective truth of the object is its application and realization in action, not its name. The 'furnished' space becomes inhabited and then deserted through the open action of the actors, envelops the audience with its atmosphere and puts it in a situation similar or analogical to that of the actors. Acting, freed from the psychological approach, forces the actor to break the monolithic part and at the same time allows for changes of personality within the same production. Scenes of noise clash against scenes of silence, scenes of laughter with scenes of tragedy, indifference with fascination. The events take place in the unknown, the barely suspected areas. We discover them in propositions other than those which can be created on the basis of knowledge. They meet on two inter-penetrating and linked planes: of reality and vision. The afunctionality of objects has, as its purpose, the visualization of the myth of our times. In the simultaneity of acting, the role of exposition is filled by images composed together with the actors. They are related to circumstances which precede the action, are its starting point, its motto or closing accent. They do not explain the sequence, but disappear with the development of action. Emerging from the action, they may appear unexpectedly, be an extension or a single moment suspended in a dying movement. They happen most often at the meeting point of two events of different form. . . .

"The prop can act as a setting or be its part. It can be used in various ways even . . . . Light forms the stage space, shines through objects. Thus the climate of the stage which resembles neither night nor day is created. While the audience is watching, light transforms the stage, changes its dimensions, its plastic arrangement. . . .

"In the structure of this theatre the world lives simultaneously in a number of functions. When declamation separates it from the rest of action—it becomes empty. This very important means of communication is subordinated to the created character. Thus, creative theatre should not limit its work to a literary interpretation of a given work. The collective creative act offers a greater possibility of expressing the complex contents of our times. A theatrical production ought to be a new quality, an independent value seen simultaneously from a number of different perspectives . . . . The theatre is capable of expressing more than can be said."

You have noticed that the cited signposts to the future theatre are confined to reconstructed performer-plus-manipulated-objects ensembles—ascetic pilgrimages back to the sources of the theatre's strength and uniqueness. This exclusion of multi-media is deliberate. Those fireworks are the World of Tomorrow only in a Flushing Meadows-Expo sense, part of the what is Good for General Motors is Good for America syndrome. The Very Latest in visual bombardment may be snappy packaging for antediluvian dramaturgical thinking—or nonthinking—because honestly, the Message Is the Message. The designer must be the super-

Howard Bay
"Love of Three Oranges"
(1939)

192

Howard Bay   "Halloween"   (1972)

scavenger, up on all the doodads peddled by the trendy outriders of the arts; but the Sermon for the Day is, Technology is the Beginning, not the End. Mechanical devices tend to get out of hand, as Dr. Frankenstein discovered, and he hadn't heard of multiple screen projection. The move is away from machines to a close examination of what is basically human in humanity. The designer's job shifts from providing information in the form of a static environment to dreaming up objects that just appear, connect with the actors in a meaningful relationship, and as quickly disappear. Objects become emblems, insignia, dynamic images. I have the feeling that Bill de Kooning's remark applies, "Forms ought to have the emotion of a concrete experience. For instance, I am very happy that grass is green."

Young designers toss and turn with a pain they cannot locate. The disturbance surfaces in a rash of Camp. Camp is different things to different people. To the fashion crowd Camp is a scratching in the cemetery to unearth an exploitable bone, to those of us with graying temples it is legal nostalgia, to the young it is a love-hate thing. This dialectic is compounded of a soft warm ache for pastoral, carefree times floating outside of history and a compulsive itch to destroy the Elders through ridicule. Unlike the film whose past is frozen for all to see, to study, to appropriate, the theatre's performance traditions evaporate

193

Peter Harvey   "Boys in the Band"   (New York, 1969)

with closing night. The New Theatre, the post-Beckett era beyond literature, is without nourishment from vanished theatrics. Destroying conventions is wild fun but new conventions must fill the breech because conventions by definition are nothing more than a language understood by actors and audiences—a floor beneath our feet. We need a bit more than the Keystone Comedies; although the madhouse frame is fitting for the 70's it is not a meaty, subtle style on which to hang the Big Dramatic Issues of Our Day. Camp is a perverse spinoff in the search for roots, but the Search itself is genuine. As luck would have it, the visual side of production can draw from the bank of pictorial history, while our friends the actors are stuck with the distortions from the plastic factories of Hollywood, U.S.A. In the firming up of precise images that will mold the New Theatre, the designer is the key. He thumbs through past art with an unclouded vision and a determination to track down salvageable antecedents. It is rather difficult to patch together a Living Tradition out of old Playbills and the memoirs of stars of yesteryear, but perhaps something will come from the art wing.

A few words on contemporary art, as wisps and shards from the galleries now and then find their way

Robin Wagner "Lenny" (New York, 1970)

Howard Bay   "My Mother, My Father and Me"   [backdrop]   (New York, 1963)

Page references for illustration

186 onstage and lend that excruciating touch of chic to the performance. Painting, the application of paint to
187 canvas with a brush, wound up its history with de Kooning. Since that day we have had various styles of decorative patterns and many objects that are really pieces of congealed art criticism. These products seem to be of vital interest to artists and to those that sell art. These demonstration-lectures in paint have been attenuated to the point of invisibility. What could be more exhilarating than a rectangle of black, or better still, a rectangle of white? The exercises were extended into three dimensions, and in time mechanical movement was added and then a bit of rudimentary electronic circuitry. They are laboriously digging up Earth in playground shapes—I am not sure how this ties in with ecology. I think we can say that the separation from human concerns in the Art Scene That Matters is well-nigh complete.

   The theatre is notoriously sluggish about keeping up with the Arts, the lag borders on unconsciousness. Who in the hell is Cezanne? He isn't listed in Players' Guide. I would like to put forward the novel proposition that the exasperating retardation isn't all bad. The rewards of drifting along outside the Now circuit are considerable: (1) One cannot be picked up today and dropped tomorrow because one Doesn't Really Count. (2) The artistic, dilettantish meddling with theatre is tempered by the crass necessity of straining to reach the ticket buying population. (3) The theatre is oblivious of the Cultural Thing as it traffics in the stew of human conflicts. This wallowing in pulsating life builds up an immunity to the lifeless constructs of the Significant Form crowd. (I know the phrase Significant Form hasn't been in vogue for ages, but what do you call the Op, Hard Edge, Minimal and Conceptual games? Insignificant Form?) (4) The theatre instinctively warms up to the Dada-Expressionist-Surrealist-Pop Art line because of its ground-

ing in human concerns—just a few illustrations from my past. The theatre may be tardy in noticing where
it's at, but the theatre's borrowings escape the emasculating, dehydrating perversions with which the
commercial art industry cannabalizes bumptious innovations. In the end a thousand dollar beaded American Indian couturier creation turns into an enemy costume in a Guatemalan street theatre. The incipient
satirical bend of Pop, which was smothered in the cradle by the fashion vampires, is reborn in recent scenic
design. The Warhol Factory shrivels to a freak boutique, but experimental groups in Brazil and Cracow
pump flesh and comment into the cartoon blow-ups.

188, 189
190, 191
192, 193

The theatre has always been a slapdash affair careening around clowns, greasepaint, sloppy sentiment and
hare-brained thinking. In just blithe!y being the last refuge of all the unsanitary goodies That Are Out Of

Wilfrid Minks "Frühlings Erwachen" (Breman, 1965)

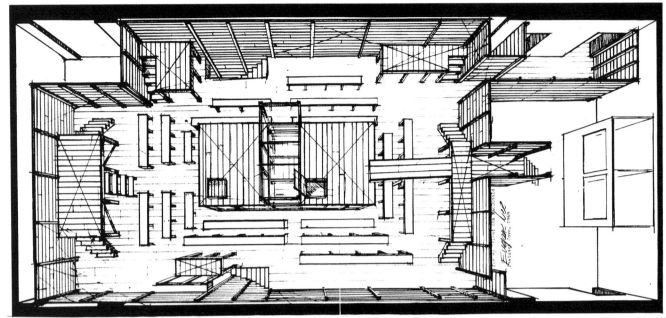

Eugene Lee "Slave Ship"
(New York, 1970)

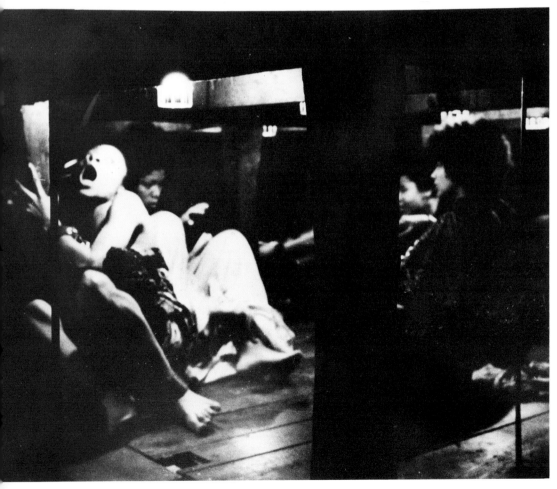

Eugene Lee "Slave Ship"
(New York, 1970)

Place In Modern Life, it has infuriated the Advanced Authorities in the Arts Today. The Pundits' Revenge is a campaign to convert the obstreperous lively actor into an abstraction, a detail, an automated unit in a juggernaut of film, strobe, sound and kinetics. We are shamefaced in our hand-woven garments beside music, painting, sculpture and architecture's push toward the shiny Abstract. The designer feels out of it; perhaps Hard Edge and the second round of Constructivism should perk up the stage. Not necessarily; the nub of Grotowski's message is let's get back to the human scale and in the process peel away the sloppy sentiment and the hare-brained thinking. The other side of the debate, the case for the Abstract, is ably put by Michael Kirby in *The Art of Time*. Kirby's demolition of moldy aesthetic theory is dandy; his sorting out of Happenings, Events and Games and his distinctions between matrixed and nonmatrixed presentations helpful. Tracing the alogical drift in the New Theatre back to John Cage's doorstep is not only historically accurate but inadvertently explains the precious, coterie flavoring of so much of the avant-garde doings. Donald Kaplan calls Kirby's deification of *Chance*, Kirby's Welfare State of the Mind.

Design for advanced theatrics is bound to the forces that push and pull our battered world. Near the top of the list is fragmentation, which snaps the continuity of tradition. History is broken up into pieces of equal value. A useful scrap is torn out of its customary context and hauled onstage to make a point and then discarded. Beauty, stylistic unity, period and geographic fidelity, and the original duty of objects are gone. What counts is the startling image hatching a new thought. Such images are patched together of any raw materials that in combination evoke the desired response—at moments a whatnot will serve better than a sheet of sparkling tin. No artifact is intrinsically superior to any other. The operative Idea is all; aesthetics is something they once studied in Departments of Philosophy. Mini or maxi scenery is also not a question; one right chunk on a stage may suffice; at other times a vast pile of debris will smother the actors because people are suffocated by their surroundings.

Collage, montage, found objects, transparency, bare platforms, exposed electrics, etc., are now the staple groceries of traditional dramatics. All these doodads turn up in the New Theatre, but Newness resides elsewhere. The Young Turks resolutely turn their backs on pictorial scenography, step out the stage door and look around at the physical world and goings-on therein. Unencumbered by aesthetic preconceptions, the designer can do his bit as a talented citizen—a disciplined visionary committed to helping to figure out the workings of human activity. The definition of scenic environment expands from a picturization of a documented locale to a fluid pattern of things impinging on the actors and coloring their behavior. 194
195
196

The available samples of tomorrow's stagecraft harbor weaknesses that must be chopped down. A simple emptying of the stage, an easy junking of the old without providing needed replacements, is a sure mark of a time of uncertainty and upheaval. Technique is stigmatized as part and parcel of the Dying Order, the decadent marketplace, and rudely abandoned. This fearless gesture willfully destroys the artist's tools for reaching and molding audiences. Weighty symposia on theatre architecture and the obsessive search for new materials is symptomatic of the flight from the painful necessity of finding visual devices for dragging blinding reality onstage. No material or technical contrivance is inherently retrogressive or progressive; it is rendered so by its use in a specific context. This simple-minded statement should be self-evident, but just note all that scaffolding erected for forward marching dramas and the absence of painted surfaces for same. And I am speaking as the culprit who dragged patented pipe scaffolding onto the New York stage in 1937. The current cliché, the jungle gym with chewed-up styrofoam attached, may or may not serve each

Escobar-Garcia "Balcony" (San Paulo, 1970)

and every drama, but underneath the theoretical reasons for its dominance, such as a world menaced by the Bomb—the Wasteland for real, there lurks a commonplace factor: American colleges don't teach aspiring designers how to paint scenery. Glossing over the appalling statistic that for years and years the only honest-to-God designer teaching design was Don Oenslager at Yale, it wasn't until the late '50s that a lone school, namely Boston University, went and hired a very adept scenic artist, Horace Armistead, who passed on his craft knowledge. So, if you can't handle paint, which is the way one naturally transcribes a large part of the visual world, you build a purist's paradise of lumber and metal. For this all that is required is a T-square, a triangle and a sharp pencil—and a swipe file heavy on tear sheets from *Domus.* The surface of our man-made world is covered with paint and to duplicate the centuries' accumulation of decoration, of textures, of deterioration and of emotive association is a rare skill that is being lost—the art of scenic painting.

Speaking of emotive associations, much avant-garde design cherishes its cool, which is a pity because the point of scenic design is to squeeze into inanimate matter the maximum emotional charge and thus underscore the meaning of the event. I venture to predict that this pose will be dated when we pass beyond

Bread and Puppet Theatre

W. Krakowski "The Old Woman Hatches" (Warsaw, 1969)

coterie experiments and tagging after the Very Latest into worthwhile minority, street and guerrilla theatre. Then there is the theatre of the Third World to be heard from. I am not equipped to hold forth on the Third World and its theatre, but required reading is Enrique Buenaventura's "Theatre and Culture" in *The Drama Review* (T-46, Winter 1970). That little essay should give you pause if you are all in a tizzy about just the right shade for those throw cushions in the second act.

The era of cosmetic theatre has not passed, but there are new stirrings in the Land. A dynamo named Ellen Stewart has done a heap of stirring throughout two hemispheres. The only safe bit of wisdom that can be handed to the design wing in preparation for a New Day is to arm oneself with all the portable, cheap handicrafts, such as celastic casting, dyeing, mask fabrication and impasto painting. The craft manuals are more helpful than the strictly theatrical textbooks, excepting *Thermoplastic Scenery for Theatre* by N. L. Bryson. The commercial compartmentalization of production will not remain, so not only will the set-costume-lighting be shouldered by one body, but more often than not the designer will build the sets, costumes and properties—and perhaps hang and run the lights. In such rugged terrain there is no place for indulgent display because every detail must hit the mark. The artist is cornered; he must think before making things. There are tough times ahead, and mother and Edward Gordon Craig didn't warn us.

The noise about visceral communication, about dim Archetypes and buried Myths, about Paradise Now, about what Artaud Really Meant is swathed in a miasma of Westchester Intellectual Upbringing; this pixie world where people actually talk about Honest Advertising and Dionysian Ritual Today must pass away. It will be a Shattering Experience to all the little Improv grouplets when the chain is pulled and even the phrase Avant Garde goes down the drain. The news flash is that young minds are fumbling with the One and Only Genuine Theatrical Question: how do we use the tools of our craft to help patch up the U.S.A., expressing that which goes unexpressed by the media Goliaths, stirring up a boisterous wind to dispel the stagnant air? Starting with the economy-size operation and the desire to meet the folks out there on their own terms with all their horrendous mental baggage of cant and prejudice is the lone path out of the cave clogged with advanced souls groping and groping 'til Doomsday. And it follows that the designer will not snicker at pop culture, but will take off from these comfy crutches of Middle America. The superior designer will then turn this cloying heritage inside out. The paraphernalia of graphics comes in play: photo blow-ups on top of darkroom tinkering with negatives; photo printing on fabrics; transparent overlays, but outsized; patterns thrown on bodies al la Nicholaus, as well as on inanimate surfaces; film and closed circuit meshed with the action; reflecting/transparent materials; portable projectors manipulated by actors; inflatable props; animated objects (self-propelled and by remote control). Now the appliances are tossed in for sheer titillation, but they can serve calculated artistic ends—just don't fall in love with the toys. The breakdown in the boundaries between man and the environment can be sharply brought home with a filmed computer operation cascading over a human body, slicing the anatomy into disjointed sections.

The overriding concern must be the human and his struggles. The designer illuminates the interaction of the actor and his physical field. Any construct builds outward from the actor and his actions, as opposed to embellishing the stage with a mannerist display of a designer's sensibility—the sculptured, architonic modeling of space is dead. The Brechtian approach falls midway between these poles. It stakes out a free acting space surrounded by side and background blackboards on which an artist chalks his pertinent comments. I find this disturbing. In their determination to shatter the soupy synthetic unity of backward drama the Brechtians segregate humanity from the environment. I *know* the theory, but I don't buy it. That is not the way things are. Actors must fight the dense, insane zone of material that smothers them.

The one inescapable fact rearing its head out of the swamp is that the theatre will contract to collectives of kindred talents who strain to reach the America that is not very interested in theatre at the moment. The designer shall be a key figure in such collectives. The economists have finally noticed that the theatre is a residual handicraft in the increasingly untenable position of economic suicide relative to the total mechanized economy. The commercial theatre can only go downhill—whatever hour the curtain goes up. We can just hope that the survivors strive to reach the American population with an updated explosion of the glamor and color that is theatre and theatre alone. We really are at the crossroads, but we no longer confront a fine old character actor impersonating the Button Molder. We face a people that might notice a New Theatre—if it is exciting.

APPENDIX I. STAGE MACHINERY
By William Cruse

A variety of mechanisms are used to erect, position, and manipulate the scenery in a modern theatre. These devices fall into three categories: hoists, lifts and horizontal drives. Hoists are used for flying scenery up to or down from the stage "penthouse"; lifts are used to bring up scenic elements from beneath the stage floor; and horizontal drives are used to slide flats, platforms, and large properties from the wings onto the visible part of the stage or from one area of the stage to another. Hoists are the most common type of mechanism in the theatre, and there are three varieties: counterbalance, electrical, and fluid drive.

The theory of a hoist is fairly simple: to life an object one needs a rope, a fixed pulley or sheave, and a man. The man provides the force needed to lift the object and the weight needed to counter the object's weight. The simplest analogy is that of a seesaw: the scenery is on one side and the stagehand is on the other. The pulley provides a stationary fulcrum with which to lift the object and a smoothly turning surface to reduce friction. If the weight of the object is greater than the pulling power of the man, he must increase his effect by adding a counterbalancing weight on his side of the final fulcrum.

The simplest method of hoisting is by counterbalancing. This type of hoist is operated by positioning a balancing weight on the hoisting line in opposition to the payload (the scenery). The stagehand operates the hoist by temporarily inducing a state of imbalance on the operating line, to raise or lower the scenery.

There are two methods of counterbalancing, the hemp system and the iron counterweight system. In the hemp system, sandbags and iron ingots are used as a counterbalance. The system uses a batten to which are attached four to six rope lines, made of first-grade manila hemp. Each line passes over its associated loft block, and then goes to the master head block sheave. There are sandbags of varying weights used to counterbalance the payload.

The second type, the iron counterweight system, is similar to the hemp system in that it also uses a batten, lines, associated loft blocks, and a master head block sheave. The lines, however, are made of wire rope instead of hemp. And the operating rope is not a free rope directly attached to the hoisting line. Rather, it is a fixed system, held between the master head block sheave and a fixed-tension sheave. For counterweighting, there is an arbor or carriage, in which the iron weights are placed. Finally, there is a lock-rail combination to ensure the safe use of the counterweights. Because of these safety features, the iron counterweight system has replaced the hemp system in modern theatres. The older system, though, has features of flexibility and operation not found in the newer systems.

Electrically powered stage hoist systems are designed to meet economic criteria not met by the counterbalance system. Electricity may be used to replace one or both functions of the man in the counterbalance hoist. It may just provide the pulling power, while still needing counterbalancing (electrical counterweight-assisted hoists), or it may provide the lifting ability and the force needed to counterbalance the weight of the object moved (pure power hoists).

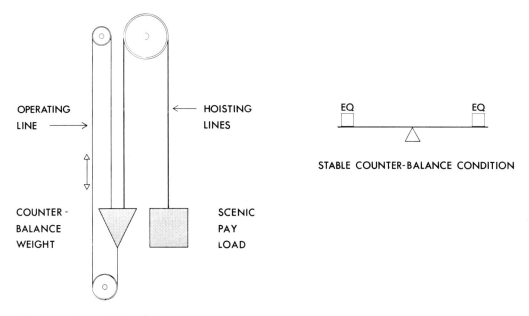

OPERATING LINE →

← HOISTING LINES

COUNTER- BALANCE WEIGHT

SCENIC PAY LOAD

EQ   EQ

STABLE COUNTER-BALANCE CONDITION

Theoretical model of a fulcrum

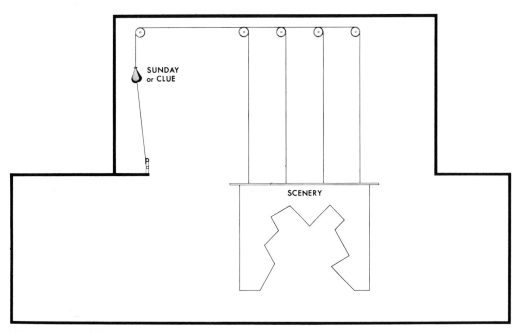

SUNDAY or CLUE

P

SCENERY

Hemp counterbalance

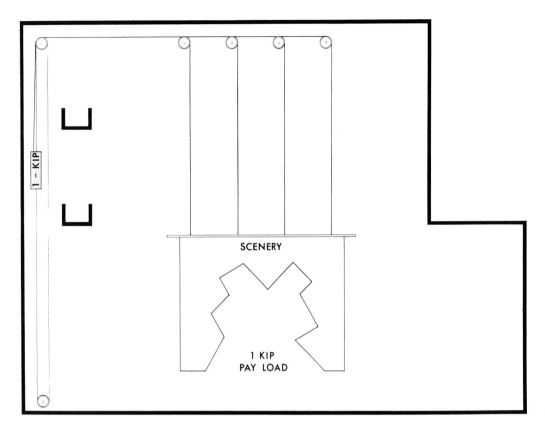

SCENERY

1 KIP
PAY LOAD

Iron counterbalance

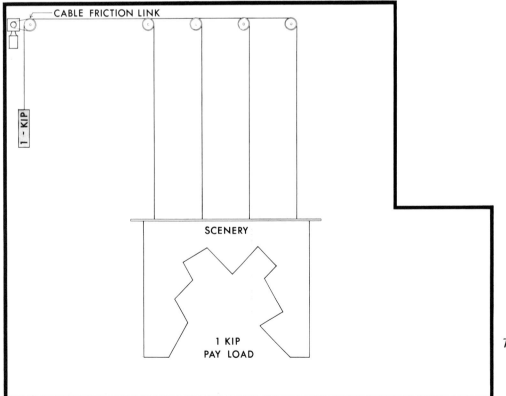

CABLE FRICTION LINK

1 - KIP

SCENERY

1 KIP
PAY LOAD

Traction drive counterweight hoist

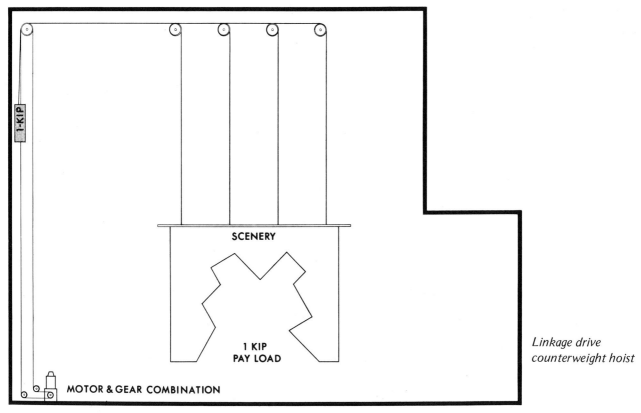

1-KIP

SCENERY

1 KIP
PAY LOAD

MOTOR & GEAR COMBINATION

*Linkage drive
counterweight hoist*

The electrical counterweight-assisted hoist closely resembles the iron counterweight system, except that an electric motor-reduction gear combination is used to provide the power to drive the counterweight carriage. In this system, a surprisingly small motor is needed to move the payload, since the payload is already counterbalanced. All the motor system need do is to overcome the inertia and friction of the counterbalance system.

There are two varieties of electrically counterweight-assisted hoists, the traction-drive type and the linkage-drive type. In the traction-drive system, the hoisting lines are passed over the associated loft blocks and then to the master head block sheave. Once past the master head block, the line is connected to the counterweights. Lifting power is provided directly to the shaft of the master head block sheave by means of an electric motor-gear reduction system.

Since the hoisting line-counterweight system is not directly coupled to the electric motor drive, an overrunning slip condition develops during acceleration and deceleration of the payload. That is, the hoisting line running over the master head block is not mechanically linked to the block itself. In that case, slippage occurs between the hoisting lines and the groove in the head block sheave. This slippage prevents completely accurate control over the entire hoisting system. The rate of slippage will vary with the weight of the payload and/or the velocity developed.

Consequently, traction-drive hoists are usually impractical for most stage uses, where the weight of the scenery varies for each production. This hoist is utilized, however, when there is a relatively constant weight being lifted at a constant velocity, such as the heavy asbestos curtains, light bridges, and orchestra shells.

The other type of counterweight-assisted electric hoist is the linkage drive. In design, it is similar to the

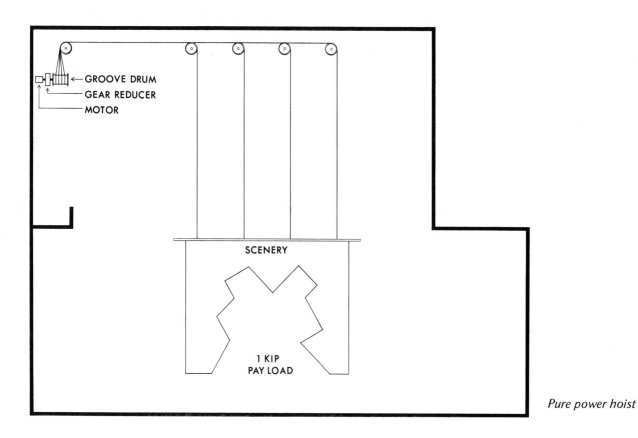

GROOVE DRUM
GEAR REDUCER
MOTOR

SCENERY

1 KIP
PAY LOAD

Pure power hoist

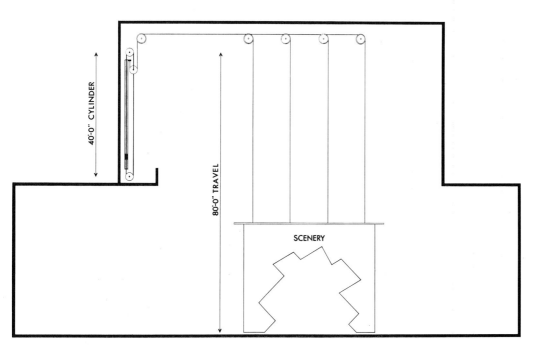

40'-0" CYLINDER

80'-0" TRAVEL

SCENERY

Fluid-drive hoist

traction-drive hoist, except that the hoisting lines are rigid metal links attached directly to the motor. The disadvantage of the traction-drive system was that a certain momentum had to be built up before the hoisting lines would catch into the grooves in the master head block sheave. In the linkage-drive system, there is no time lapse between the start of the motor and the movement of the hoisting line, because the line is already attached to the motor.

The second category of electric hoist is the pure power in contrast to the counterweight-assisted type. The pure power hoist is composed of a motor, usually placed on a gridiron, a brake, a gear reducer, and a drum around which several hoisting lines wind. This motor must be of greater capacity than those in the counterweight-assisted systems, for it not only provides the power to balance the hoisted payload but also replaces the entire counterweight arbor. In simple terms, this motor is now providing the load pressure for both sides of the seesaw. The variable-speed motor and gear-reducer combination prevent a jerking motion of the load when the motor is turned on or off.

The disadvantages of the pure power system are: (1) it is expensive because of the variable-speed motor, (2) it weighs more than the counterweight-assisted system because of the need for a higher horsepower motor reducer combination to replace the counterweights, and (3) it takes up more space backstage.

The best-known example of a pure power system is installed at the Metropolitan Opera House in New York, where there are 110 motors linked into a single console that can be run by a single operator. Another disadvantage in this system, important when comparing it with the fluid-drive hoists, is that the electricity needed to operate several motors at once cannot be divided at will among a greater number of motors. In plain language, a motor is either on or off; it cannot use half of its electricity and return the unused half to the source, to be passed on to another motor. What happens backstage is the amount of electricity needed to run ten motors at full power cannot be altered to run twenty motors at half power.

The third type of hoist is the fluid-drive system. An analogy to this type is an electric water pump, which generates the power to move the water up the pipe, where the water acts directly to push the food off the plate in the sink. In the fluid-drive hoist, an electric generator is used to run a fluid (water, oxygen, air or other fluid) piston, which in turn moves the hoisting lines.

The advantages of this system are several, and they are significant in terms of theatre architecture. One of the principal advantages is the fact that the electric generator does not have to be anywhere near the fluid drive; it can be placed in the air-conditioning room of the theatre, for example. Because the fluid-drive part of the hoist is noiseless, and an electric generator is not, the audience no longer has to listen to the motor driving the hoists in motion. Also, the electric generator of the fluid-drive system does not have to take up valuable floor space backstage. The most important benefit of the fluid-drive system is that the operator may split the power between any number of pistons. In other words, although electricity cannot be divided, the power generated by a fluid can be.

Lifts are used in the theatre to vertically propel various production elements, such as platforms, actors, and scenery, above or below the stage floor. In contrast to the hoist, which is supported by the "over-stage" structure, the lift is supported and guided by the stage floor and/or the cellar floor below the stage. The two general types of lifts are the architecturally integrated and the temporary production apparatus.

Architecturally integrated lifts are designed in accordance with local building safety codes; in New York, for instance, only direct plungers and screw-jack actuators can be built into a theatre. A direct plunger lift is

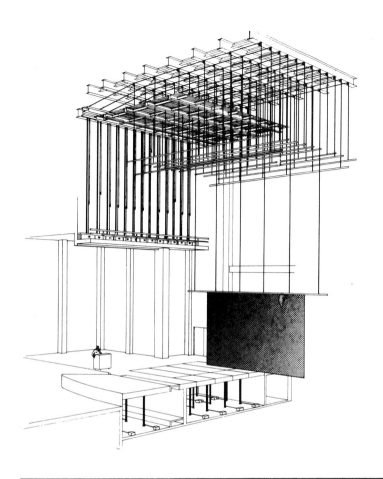

Architecturally integrated lifts

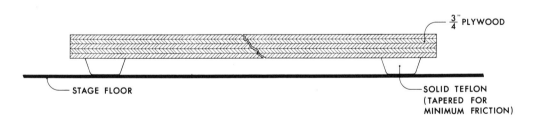

$\frac{3}{4}$" PLYWOOD

STAGE FLOOR

SOLID TEFLON
(TAPERED FOR
MINIMUM FRICTION)

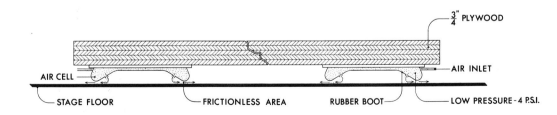

$\frac{3}{4}$" PLYWOOD

AIR CELL

AIR INLET

STAGE FLOOR — FRICTIONLESS AREA — RUBBER BOOT — LOW PRESSURE - 4 P.S.I.

*Teflon and air-cell
horizontal drives*

hydraulically driven, using a piston attached to a portion of the stage floor. The piston operates under hydraulic pressure (like the pure power hoist), and is expanded and collapsed to effectively elevate the associated platform. The screw-actuated lift is either electrically or hydraulically driven, and coupled to a vertical screw through a nut in which the upper end of the screw is connected to a portion of the stage floor.

The layout and installation of permanent architecturally integrated lifts must be carefully determined by the envisioned frequency of use, the type of events to be accommodated, and the attendant inflexibility of the permanent mechanization of the stage floor. In general, architecturally integrated lifts are successfully employed where the scene designer of a permanent resident company has defined the geometry of the lifts to meet the specific production needs of the company.

Horizontal drives are used to rotate, propel and project scenery, actors, properties, etc., from the off-stage areas onto the acting area. In an effort to meet the audience demand for rapidly changing scenery, designers often utilize a system of horizontally moving platforms. Although the articulation of horizontal motion on the stage is unlimited, there are several established configurations that are easily identifiable: the "wing-to-wing" classical opera wagon, the jackknife arrangement, the revolve or turntable, the treadmill, and the revolving segment.

A horizontal drive is composed of two elements, the load-bearing device and a horizontal actuator. The bearing device, such as wheels or casters, reduces the friction between the load and the floor, allowing the scenery to be moved with minimum force. Among the newest types of bearing devices are plastic-teflon glides and air cells.

A word of caution on the importation of sophisticated, nontheatrical mechanisms. Unlike the traditional lumber and simple metal contrivances, advanced electrical gear must be precisely engineered, installed by experts and handled by trained personnel.

APPENDIX II. LIGHTING CONTROLS
By Ralph Holmes

Controls are the machinery for varying light intensities. Instruments are grouped together to provide a wash of light from various directions (back light or cross light) and in appropriate colors (cool or warm, saturated or pale) to suit the action, mood and atmosphere. Other individual units are controlled as specials and used to isolate or highlight the action. Most shows require a blend of washes and specials. It is rare for a production to use only specials; the pile-up of specials creates a coverage but with strange overlaps and mixtures of color.

The old workhorse of the professional theatre, road tour and summer stock is the cumbersome but reliable "piano" switchboard. This antique resistance dimmerboard has not changed since 1914. It is a

CBS-SCR portable console

CBS-SCR portable dimmer rack

monstrous, inefficient, mechanical contraption that, with clever manipulation, tedious hours of lighting rehearsal and brute strength, can be coaxed into creating interesting effects—but at a staggering cost of time and effort.

One of the practical assets of a portable dimmerboard set-up, with its associated plug boxes and preset boards, is flexibility. During tryouts or on tour or settling down in a permanent house, the requirements of the production will be modified. Advance theatre booking allows the designer to plan ahead for the tightest spots. Still, the production electrician may end up in the basement, on the fly floor or halfway out in the back alley. For the most part, the operating production electrician seldom sees the stage and works all his cues blind.

For anyone who has not grappled with basic electricity in summer stock, using a pair of piano switch-boards, or has never manipulated anything but a ten preset electronic control board in his community or university theatre, a short rundown will help evaluate the crude practicality and flexibility of this basic switchboard. The training acquired performing cues in a totally manual operation is of help in learning basic control techniques.

The piano dimmerboard can be used alone as a functioning unit, but it has two auxiliaries: the plugging boxes, which serve as a patch panel, and the preset board of smaller wattage dimmers. The average portable dimmerboard weighs about 800 pounds, is castered for portability, is covered for protection in transit, and can be hefted by four men. The internal wiring and the temporary installation to the house panel meet all electrical and fire codes. The majority of these boards are still equipped with resistance dimmers so that they can be used in the older houses where DC current is all that is available. A limited number of auto transformer boards are to be had, but the tour's itinerary must be limited to theatres that have been modernized with a supply of AC current. At the inception of dimmer control, most of the older theatres had been wired long before with DC current for arc follow spots—and have never changed. DC is still found in the projection booth for arc follow spots and projectors.

The most common portable boards consist of either fourteen 3000-watt or twelve 5000-watt resistance dimmers. The entire board is fused and controlled by one large, three-bladed knife switch. Each dimmer circuit in turn is controlled by one knife switch with a pair of fuses, and terminates in one porcelain stage pocket. Each dimmer has a single handle that can be moved independently or interlocked with a mechanical master. As a rule, the allotment of circuits, aside from borderlights, works in combinations of two, four or six circuits. The twelve-plate board was made to accommodate borderlites in three or four circuits. Both boards are wired with a single phase-three wire master, which means that either outside leg and a neutral

Computer (with electric typewriter)

Computer (with light pencil)

will deliver 110 volts. The board will also work on a house set-up that consists of three phase, four wire, merely by using two outside legs and a neutral from the house panel.

Portable boards are available with a double throw switch for each dimmer and two stage pockets, one for each side of the double throw switch. Without repatching during a hectic show, it is possible to control special groups of lighting equipment that do not overlap—that will not both be used at the same time. For example: in the upthrow, a single dimmer may control four units that are used for a special limbo area stage right. In the downthrow, this same dimmer may control four units that cover a special limbo area stage left. And there is the catch, for at no time can both areas be used together; you are stuck with your choice. And during a busy show, woe betide the busy operator that doesn't have all his upthrows and downthrows in correct sequence, let alone the dimmer handles and preset boards. The individual dimmer handles can be interlocked or "picked," in any combination into the master handle. Those handles not interlocked will remain at their readings. In a slow cue it is possible to unlock, or unpick, individual handles at different readings, while those still interlocked progress to a higher or lower reading. The reverse, of course, is possible: to pick several handles that are at different readings so that they will automatically lock into the master handle as it moves. The main switch used to activate the board may also be used for total blackouts. Wire the single 60-watt worklight on the board on the hot side so you won't be in the dark.

The plug box is a means of controlling groups of units where no preset is required, because all units will dim together to the same level at the same speed. It can also be used for regrouping or repatching between a sequence of cues. Replugging can be done within the box for individual units, or the entire box controlling a group of units can be unplugged and exchanged for another. The plug box itself is an enclosed box with a lead of eight feet terminating in a full-stage plug. The enclosed portion contains four or six porcelain stage pockets, each pocket internally fused. In operation, the plug boxes are usually stacked upright in a row on top of the portable board in sequence corresponding to the dimmer into which each is patched. One full stage plug or two half plugs can be inserted into each full porcelain pocket.

The preset board is in essence a single preset. It adds greatly to the flexibility of the portable board in performing a sequence of cues as well as providing a refinement of readings. The preset board is itself a small dimmerboard. In principle, six 500-watt dimmers, or four 750-watt dimmers with individual handles and pockets are grouped electrically with one lead to plug into a 3000-watt dimmer on the larger portable board. The portable board serves as a master control, each dimmer proportionally overriding the individual readings of the group of smaller dimmers patched into it. The preset boards come in groups of twelve 500-watt dimmers, and 750-watt dimmers, subdivided in half with two leads—two groups in each board to

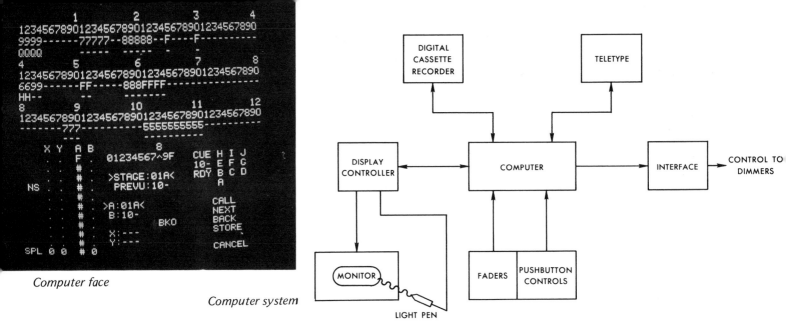

Computer face

Computer system

save space, each group totaling 3000 watts. Also available is a six-unit board; six 1000-watt dimmers divided into two groups with two leads. Since the maximum load capacity of the 5000-watt plate is actually 6000 watts, both leads for any of these preset boards can be patched into a single 5000-watt dimmer. A versatile tool when one considers the wattages available today, particularly in ellipsoidal spotlights. With properly organized light plot the designer can assign a single dimmer to each special unit and still have overall proportional control.

A special area can be lighted with four 750-watt ellipsoidal spotlights; one directly overhead on stage or as a back light, a second on the balcony rail, and one each on the box booms left and right. By patching these four units into a preset board they can be individually balanced with the 750-watt plates in the preset board, as well as controlled as a group by a 3000-watt dimmer plate on the master board. Also, readings can be preset for individual units between cues. It is still only one preset, but with nimble hands, elbows, knees and feet, and a few short lengths of batten, one man can work a flock of cues.

Another item of equal backbreaking bulk and weight is cable, the long runs of individual cables that are tied in neat, heavy bundles and used to power each and every instrument. You can recognize it on the balcony rail because it snakes a devious route along the ornamental plasterwork toward the backstage switchboards. Gradually some theatres have installed a fairly adequate number of permanent outlets along the balcony rail and for the box booms. This outlay of money by the management is spent to meet the local fire codes as well as to qualify for better insurance rates. All the new theatres are being built with such outlets available out front; however, backstage there is nothing.

No theatres are identical, old or new; so what you find in New Haven or New York you may not find in Boston, Philadelphia or Wilmington. To meet all conditions, the production electrician carefully lays out in the shop, tests and labels neatly tied bundles of individual cables for the balcony rail, the box booms and all of the "production electric" pipes on stage. The total length of the runs will be determined by the most extreme distance to be encountered on tour (including the final, inaccessible corner allotted to the switchboards). In New Haven the switchboards may be on stage right—on the fly floor two flights up. The next stop, Boston, will find the switchboards on stage right again, but at the stage floor level. When you settle down to the run in New York, the switchboards as well as all the cable runs may be reversed to stage left—and back on the fly floor again. So include an electric chain hoist in the work box. Your production electrician should have a private collection of blueprints of the major theatres, which he has gathered over the years.

While Broadway lingers behind, new theatres have arisen across the country in the universities, community theatres and new cultural centers. Many of them are the equal of the model theatres rebuilt in Europe since World War II. What these theatres have in common is the use of electronic systems for the remote control of lighting, as contrasted to the banks of resistance or auto transformer dimmers that were installed twenty years ago. Research and development of the pure thyratron dimmer by George Izenour at Yale University in 1948 brought continuous and instantaneous control to remote systems for the first time. Aside from the direct simplicity of operation, his design gave the lighting designer the additional facility for an "infinite" system of preset cues as an integral concept of his system. It now became practical to install the control console at a vantage point in the auditorium so that the lighting designer and operator could see every nuance and change in the sequence of light cues.

Today, the thyratron dimmers are being replaced by the new developments in SCR dimmers. The silicon rectifier is a transistorlike device; it handles heavy currents and performs in the same manner as the thyratron tube. Whereas silicon rectifiers, combined with the saturable reactor, act as a one-way passage allowing electrons to flow only in one direction, the silicon controlled rectifier gates the flow of power, resulting in high efficiency. The advantages of SCR dimmer are: compact size, low weight, low cost, instantaneous response, high efficiency, and long life. The stability of the SCR dimmer makes it ideal for trouping.

CBS television has developed a unitized-modular system of SCR dimmer racks with a five-scene preset console. All the components are stock items, are available commercially, and the entire system is intended for trouping. It has been used as a temporary installation or as a semi-permanent installation in a theatre or studio. Several Ice Shows travel year round with SCR equipment assembled and built to suit their needs. The Metropolitan Opera on tour uses racks of portable SCR dimmers and a control console. The practical solution for all types of productions is a unitized system built of interchangeable parts, where every component as well as an entire assembly of units is interchangeable. And with such a system actually at hand, we have a suitable replacement for the old piano boards. The secondary benefit is greater flexibility in lighting equal to the quality available in a permanent studio installation.

The system is comprised of portable dimmer racks and a five-scene preset console. The dimmer racks hold six 12,000-watt SCR dimmers, identical in size, and interchangeable. Smaller wattage dimmers may be substituted, although they will require the identical amount of space. The control console has provision for twenty-four dimmer controls with a manual and five presets. Four racks of dimmer are provided for a single console. Two control consoles joined together, electrically and mechanically, provide forty-eight dimmer circuits or eight racks of dimmers. It is possible to join three or four consoles together for a large operation. The racks of dimmers can be aligned side by side, or stacked in two or three tiers. Between the dimmer racks and the control console runs a thin signal cable made of standard 12-volt multicable, which provides the great versatility of the entire system. Since its length can run from a few feet to several thousand, the control console can be positioned anywhere backstage, in the front of the house or even outside the building proper. It has been used in the temporary control room of a television remote bus that was parked around the corner from the stage.

The outstanding practical aspect of the entire system centers around the positioning of the dimmer racks. It is not necessary to stack them all in one location; in fact, it is preferable to distribute the racks in positions nearest to the lighting positions, cutting down on the long runs of individual cables. The dimmer racks that control the box booms and balcony rail can be placed out in the house in a corner. The power cables, instead of the usual bundle of individual cables that in turn feed the racks, are run to the backstage power source. Other racks can be positioned wherever needed, such as in the tormenters, on the fly floor or in the cellar—whatever location provides the shortest run to the lighting equipment. So between each dimmer rack and the control console runs the thin signal cable (one from each rack) converging on the control console.

A limit of six dimmers to a rack was chosen because a rack of six dimmers is a convenient size to handle and it is small enough to go through a narrow door, or to fit into a small elevator. In an emergency it can fit into a station wagon or an airplane. It can be hoisted up several stories on a block and fall, or motorized chain hoist, and swung through a loading door or window. It is also small enough to be stacked one atop another. A rack of twelve to fifteen dimmers reaches the same bulk, if not weight, of the old piano boards, which never could be stacked in a tight corner. A final advantage to a dimmer rack of six 12,000 SCR dimmers is that the electrical load per rack is identical to the larger piano boards: a 200-amp service, four wire, three phase. The feed cables for the racks are flexible welding cable with watertight camlock connectors—each color-coded. The SCR dimmer units are totally interchangeable; each one is fused separately with a circuit breaker. An internal fan provides air circulation as soon as the power leads are connected to the house panel. In this way air cooling is provided before the dimmers are turned on, and continues to function after the board has been turned off.

Female inputs for patching into the racks are of a pin-connector type for simplicity. The dimmer rack provides a patch system of two 60-amp female pin connectors for each dimmer. Obviously, with correct tags on each cable it is possible to repatch. Groups of instruments can be ganged together on the production pipes with multiple connectors in the conventional way. Actually a more elaborate portable patch system is available as well as a rigid patch rack similar to the cross-patch panels used in permanent installations. A lot depends upon the complexity of the production and the time allotted for the setup. For a large production the heavy individual cable runs can be further simplified by the use of multicable and portable "light battens" that are, essentially, small conduits with a limited number of outlets. It comes close to a permanent conduit installation with fixed outlets at specified intervals. Each batten has four 30-amp pin-connector outlets. This will provide power for twelve 1000-watt units, four 3000-watt or 2000-watt units, or paired, two 5000-watt units. The battens are five feet in length and hang on a production pipe with two standard C clamps. The multicable comes in lengths of twenty-five, fifty and one hundred feet, and can be interconnected to make up various runs. The plugging box for the multicable system provides power for two such cables, or the capacity of two 12,000-watt dimmers. The multicable provides four individual cables to match the four outlets on the batten. When the multicable is patched into the plugging box, four male connectors are provided to match each circuit of the multicable.

In the same plugging box, but independent, is a large male pin connector that patches into a 12,000-watt dimmer. At the plugging box end, this main cable terminates into four female outlets. Each circuit has a 30-amp circuit breaker at the rear of the plugging box. Actually two units have been combined into one. A feed from the dimmer supplies four female outlets; and the multicable supplies four circuits with four male pin connectors. Together they comprise a cross-patch system. The fact that they are combined into one box merely simplifies the number of units.

There is also a studio-type cross-patch panel. It provides inputs for the multicable as well as inputs for the dimmers. Cross-patching is done with simple plug-type patch cords—male and female, so that no one can patch one dimmer into another. Obviously this type of central patch panel requires that all the dimmer racks be positioned in one location. It is perfect for a permanent installation in a rented studio or theatre where a full-scale permanent installation is not economically reasonable.

The portable control console has five banks of presets. The first preset bank can be worked independently as a manual or as a preset. For each preset there is a single fader handle. All five fader handles can be used at the same time to produce a *pile-on* effect. All five can be faded out together with a master handle.

In manual operation each dimmer can be switched from the preset mode to independent, or into a group sub-master (A, B, C or D). For each sub-master group, there is a single fader handle, and all five can be used at the same time. All four sub-masters are in turn controlled by a master fader handle. Meanwhile, those dimmers working in an independent mode are all in turn controlled by an independent master handle.

The sub-masters are handy for controlling cyc lighting separately from the presets. For a small five-scene preset console, this alternative for small and continuous changes in cyc lighting leaves the bulk of the large lighting changes in the presets, especially when the cues come fast and involve many dimmers. The independent position is handy for special cues that involve only one dimmer, such as projections or follow spots. The bulk of the show can then be run with the presets—or perhaps a small computer.

The design of lighting control boards is no longer a simple problem of electrical engineering in which the only concern is engineering requirements or code specifications. The lighting designer was left to make the most of whatever the engineers had given him. Times have changed.

The modern remote lighting control console gives the lighting designer a flexible, artistic tool. No longer is there any reason for the mechanism to interfere with the lighting.

One sophisticated tool is still missing, however—a truly "infinite" system of presets; that is, a memory bank to store all the cues of any number of productions. As practical and functional as the mechanical side of the ten preset console may be in ease of operation, there is the need for the storage of cues. Various systems of punch cards, read-out cards, tapes, memory cores have been evolved that have been so over-complicated as to get in the way of the lighting; and worse, no one can tell where they are until they have been there. All cues were lost in a limbo of mystery until they actually happened, or did not happen—and then it is too late.

With the older ten preset system, the operator can always turn immediately to the particular dimmer of the preset in question and physically check the reading. He can see the actual value of the dimmer reading as well as every dimmer value in the entire preset. The great drawback of all current systems is the lack of total visual readout of all circuits. Somewhere it is there on the card or tape—but not visible. In some systems, this has been solved by means of an instant read-out, but only for one individual dimmer at a time and by then it is too late. A total visual display of all dimmer values in each cue (whether the cue is in actual operation, or in a preview mode), is the only intelligent solution.

Today we have a new television studio installation. The heart of the system, which has been incorporated into an existing electronic switchboard, is a small, general purpose computer that has been functioning for over two years with great success. The basic memory system is the small computer. The console consists of a large television monitor upon which the cues are annotated with a "light pencil." Four fader handles control any sequence of overlapping cues. It can be interfaced with any current electronic dimming equipment and eliminates the need for an expansive array of control levers. Any number of display monitors can be installed at strategic locations to monitor cues. The unique value of this system is that every dimmer and its functioning value is in constant display at all times. During a cross fade between two cues, every value change is indicated. Cues normally follow in sequence; however, additional cues can be inserted between cues or canceled. The operator can jump forward or backward at his discretion. Any dimmer can be manually reset while in automatic operation during a performance. Cues can be activated as fast as the lamp filaments will respond. A long sequence of cues can be done in tempo to the beat of music, or slowly fading several cues at different speeds.

As for the number of cues available for storage and recall, it is generous. Assuming that a lighting console has 100 dimmers, the memory bank of the computer is able to store from 400 to 2400 cues by disk memory, or 5000 cues on tape memory, or 300 to 5000 cues on a combination of core-tape. For library storage purposes, an electric typewriter will provide printed copy of the cue sheets directly from the computer. Cartridge tape memory will provide for long-term storage, say, on a season-to-season basis.

In addition to the simplicity and directness of operation, the console is interesting to operate. It has a certain "live" quality. The total display of dimmer values and cue sequences on the monitor screen change in concert with the actual light changes on stage. It is almost as if the operator were seeing a bank of dimmer levers actually move mechanically by themselves.

One of the first, startling, visual displays occurs during a cross fade between two presets. There is no halfway dip in light levels in the middle of a cross fade, such as normally occurs in all systems to date. It is no longer necessary to fade up the second preset three quarters of the way, before fading down the first preset. The computer automatically correlates the reading of every dimmer in both presets. If dimmer 1 is at a reading of full in both presets, it remains full throughout the entire duration of the cross fade. It does not dip to half as the fader handle reaches the half-way mark between the two presets. If dimmer 2 is at a reading of 10, or full, in the first preset, and at a reading of 7 in the second—the change in light level will be a continuous dim from a reading of 10 to 7—no dips or bounces.

In addition to the automatic hold feature between presets, cues can be accumulated or "piled on" without limit. During automatic operation, instant access for emergency manual resetting of any dimmer is direct and requires no preparatory actions. The sequence of cues can be easily altered during rehearsal or performance. Any cue can be instantly previewed and reset during automatic operation. Additional cues may be inserted in the middle of an existing sequence without renumbering the previously stored cues. Cues may be canceled with total freedom.

Since the heart of the system is a small, general purpose computer about the size of a large suitcase, it can be moved or trouped along with the rest of the production. The flexibility and adaptability of the computer system are not confined to lighting. It can be programmed for other theatre operations: automated fly systems, stage wagons, turntables, sound systems and special effects. Since small, general purpose computers are not built to special order, they come in a price range that is surprisingly competitive.

This computer system is called Autocue. When first demonstrated, the signal cables were unplugged from the control consoles and plugged into the computer; and the portable system was then run by the computer. The production electrician of the theatre, who had been operating the control console, learned the complete operation of the computer system in half an hour.

ACKNOWLEDGEMENTS

Must straightaway acknowledge the work of my collaborators—busy people who Came Through: my long-time associate, Ralph Holmes, designer and CBS-TV Lighting Director who not only wrote the Appendix on lighting controls but furnished the data on projections; and William Cruse, Technical Consultant for New York's Uris Theatre Complex and the New Orleans Cultural Center. Arnold Abramson, Chargeman Scenic Artist at Nolan Studios contributed the scenic painting material.

Gold stars to each and every one at the American office of the International Theatre Institute: Rosamond Gilder, Martha Wadsworth, Judith Leabo, Elizabeth Burdick and Peggy Hansen; to Paul Myers and his staff at the Lincoln Center Library of the Performing Arts; to Louis Rachow, Librarian of The Players; to Helen Willard, Curator of Harvard's Theatre Collection; to all my fellow designers who had to scrounge through old files and portfolios; to my editor-publisher, Ralph Pine, who was more sensitive and efficient than is usual in this line of work.

"Le Theatre en Pologne" granted permission for the reprinting of Ludwik Flaszen's "After the Avant Garde" and excerpts from the interview with Josef Szajna; the Citadel Press the quotation from *Bertolt Brecht: His Art, His Life, and His Times* by Frederic Ewen; the New York Graphic Society the Leon Bakst quote from *Art and the Stage in the Twentieth Century,* Henning Rischbieter, Editor.

For the photos I am indebted to: Fred Fehl, Ulrich Franzen and Associates, Robert Galbraith, Peter A. Juley and Son, Arwid Lagenpusch, Louis Melancon, Nathan Rabin, Deidi Von Schaewen, Gerd Schulthess, E. Fred Sher, Jurgen Simon, Martha Swope, Reg Wilson and Gabriele Winter.

ABOUT HOWARD BAY

Howard Bay has designed 150 Broadway productions for which he has received two Antoinette Perry, a Maharam, a Variety Drama Critics and two Donaldson Awards. Among his credits are *Man of La Mancha; Toys in the Attic; Music Man; The Little Foxes* (both the original and the Mike Nichols revival); *Desperate Hours; The Shrike; Show Boat; Uncle Harry; One Touch of Venus; Carmen Jones; The Eve of St. Marks; one third of a nation; Up in Central Park; Something for the Boys, The Wall; The Fifth Column; Brooklyn, U.S.A.; Come Back, Little Sheba; Autumn Garden; The Children's Hour; The Patriots; Magdalena; Flahooley/Jollyanna; Regina; The Cool World; Red Roses for Me;* and *Sandhog*. He directed Bobby Clark in *As the Girls Go* and the American premieres of Mario Fratti's *The Cage*, John Arden's *Workhouse Donkey*, and Strindberg's *There Are Crimes and Crimes*; was Production Designer on such films as Doug Fairbank's *The Exile* and Balanchine's *Midsummer Night's Dream*; television Art Director on *The Pueblo* and many of the Hallmark, Omnibus and Maugham series. President of the United Scenic Artists, Board member of the National Society of Interior Designers, on the Advisory Council of the International Theatre Institute, a recipient of a Guggenheim Fellowship, Mr. Bay now holds the Alan King Chair in Theatre Arts at Brandeis University, having taught at Yale, Carnegie-Mellon, Ohio, Purdue and Oregon. Mr. Bay wrote the Staging and Stage Design section for the *Encyclopaedia Britannica*, mounted a one-man show at the Lincoln Center Astor Gallery and a touring exhibit under the auspices of the American Theatre Association.